HOSHIN KANRI

Yoji Akao
Author and Editor-in-Chief
Tamagawa University, Japan

Introduction by Greg Watson
Director of Corporate Quality,
Compaq Computer Corp.

Translated by Glenn H. Mazur
and Japan Business Consultants, Ltd.

Productivity Press
NEW YORK, NEW YORK

HOSHIN KANRI

Policy Deployment
for Successful TQM

Productivity Press

CRC Press
Taylor & Francis Group
6000 Broken Sound Parkway NW, Suite 300
Boca Raton, FL 33487-2742

© 2004 by Taylor & Francis Group, LLC
CRC Press is an imprint of Taylor & Francis Group

No claim to original U.S. Government works
Printed in the United States of America on acid-free paper
15 14 13 12 11 10 9 8
International Standard Book Number-13: 978-1-56327-301-8 (Softcover)
Library of Congress catalog number: 2004009539
Cover design by Gary Raggaglia. Art creation by Lorraine Millard

Library of Congress Cataloging-in-Publication Data

Catalog record is available from the Library of Congress

Visit the Taylor & Francis Web site at
http://www.taylorandfrancis.com

and the CRC Press Web site at
http://www.crcpress.com

Contents

NOTE: Due to the format requirements of the illustrations, many of which are two-page spreads, you will occasionally find a blank page. Please note that these are intentional, and that there is no material missing from the book.

Tables and Figures

APPENDIX

Publisher's Message

Dr. Yoji Akao, chairman and professor at Tamagawa University's Department of Industrial Engineering, has been a primary architect in the design of several quality control methodologies, including quality function deployment and policy deployment (*hoshin kanri*). Productivity Press published his edited volume, *Quality Function Deployment: Integrating Customer Requirements into Product Design*, in 1990. This year we are extremely pleased to offer our readers this latest of his works, *Hoshin Kanri: Policy Deployment for Successful TQM*.

This book provides an in-depth examination of the implementation of *hoshin kanri*, including several case studies written by the implementing companies themselves. Two of the contributing authors, Mr. Nomi and Mr. Koura, join in a conversation with Professor Akao in the last chapter, providing an intimate view of methodology design in-process. The quality movement is an evolutionary process, an example itself of continuous improvement in action. Professor Akao's book, now in English, makes it possible for Western managers to join in and contribute their own discoveries to this vital methodology.

The term *hoshin kanri* has many English equivalents created by practitioners in an attempt to capture the essence of this practice. The most frequently used terms — management by policy, hoshin planning, and policy deployment — all fall short of the complete meaning of the Japanese term and the methodology it stands for. Perhaps the most accurate term for *hoshin kanri* would be target-means deployment, but the dryness of that fails to capture the power of this method. *Hoshin* means shining metal, compass, or pointing the direction; *kanri* means management or control. *Hoshin* is often translated as policy, but it refers to something more far reaching, like the vision, purpose, or long-term direction of the company. *Hoshin kanri* is a method devised to capture and concretize strategic goals as well as flashes of insight about the future and develop the means to bring these into reality. In this book, we have kept the Japanese term, *hoshin kanri*, to indicate its unique intention: to integrate an entire organization's daily activities with its long-term goals.

With *hoshin kanri*, insight and vision are not lost, plans are not rolled up on the charts of week-long planning meetings and forgotten until next year. The daily crush of events and quarterly bottom-line pressures do not take precedence over strategic plans, rather, these short-term activities are determined and managed by the plans themselves. There is a continual process of checking to make sure that what is done each day reflects the intentions, the targets, the vision the company has agreed to pursue. Both planning and deployment are critical features of *hoshin kanri*, but in this book there is an emphasis on the deployment process itself — the development of targets, the development of means to achieve targets, and the deployment of both. Thus, we have also decided to use the most common term, *policy deployment*, to underscore this aspect of deployment that Akao emphasizes.

Hoshin kanri is one of the pillars of TQM. In Japan TQC refers to the company-wide use of quality control as well as the commitment to quality as a company strategy. In the West, TQM is the equivalent of TQC in Japan. In this book, wherever historical material appears about the development of the quality movement in Japan, TQC is maintained, otherwise we have substituted TQM. In Appendix 2, which traces the history of the development of *hoshin kanri*, the integral relationship between TQC and *hoshin kanri* is evident — the latter being the glue that pulled the former into a complete methodology rather than a collection of quality control tools.

At the heart of TQM is the PDCA cycle. This also forms the core of *hoshin kanri*, but the order is rearranged. In *hoshin kanri* one begins with the check cycle — PDCA becomes the CAPD cycle. Thus, checking the current status of company activity propels the hoshin process. With each repetition of the companywide check, a new deployment of target and means occurs at every level. Control items (control points for target deployment and checkpoints for means deployment) are integral to *hoshin kanri* implementation, and Akao gives considerable space to explaining their use. Through the CAPD, daily control — integral to the application of quality control tools in maintaining improved standards — is linked to company strategy through *hoshin kanri*.

Two other methods introduced here and necessary for the successful implementation of *hoshin kanri* are cross-functional management (CFM) and "catchball." CFM requires a structural change in management relationships and allows continuous checking of target and means throughout the product development and production processes. CFM and *hoshin kanri* enhance each other. CFM is a necessary structural addition for *hoshin kanri* (and TQM) to succeed. And *hoshin kanri* gives CFM the context within which to succeed.

Catchball is a critical process to *hoshin kanri* success also. It refers to the commitment to continual communication that is essential to the development of realistic targets and means and to their deployment at every level of the company. Feedback systems must be put in place to break down linear communication flows and allow for bottom-up, top-down, horizontal, multi-directional communication about targets, means, and their deployment progress. In order to establish such a communication system there must already be in the company a commitment to total employee involvement and an understanding of the crucial role each employee plays in the continuous improvement process.

Chapter 6 is structured around a conversation between Koura, Nomi, and Akao — the major architects of *hoshin kanri* in Japan. We have put it last because it provides a good summary of all the ingredients to successful hoshin. However, we recommend that you also read it quickly before beginning the book. Though many of the explanations won't be completely clear until you have read through the book, the conversation provides a good introduction to Akao's method and to the central issues addressed by *hoshin kanri*.

We are very grateful to Yoji Akao for the opportunity to republish his valuable book in English. We also extend our thanks to Bob King of GOAL/QPC for the translation. Glenn H. Mazur, Japan Business Consultants, Ltd., gave freely of his time to clarify questions about the original content meaning and aided in our communication with Professor Akao whenever necessary. Our gratitude to him is considerable.

Greg Watson's introduction to the book provides Western readers a context for understanding *hoshin kanri*. He clarifies the critical elements of *hoshin kanri*, offering readers a generic approach to implement this powerful methodology. We are particularly grateful to Mr. Watson for agreeing to do this on short notice. We are also pleased to announce that Productivity Press will be publishing a series of books by him in 1992, including a book on *hoshin kanri* as it has been applied in Western companies.

We also extend our thanks to all those whose efforts contributed to the high quality of this book: our production team of David Lennon, Susan Cobb, Gayle Joyce, Michele Saar and Karla Tolbert; Joyce Weston for the cover design; Christine Carvajal for copy editing, and Jennifer Cross for the index.

Preface

Management in industry today operates in an extremely harsh business climate. Many industries are engaged in structural improvement simply to survive. They are making strategic long-term and medium-term plans and implementing related policy deployment and controls. In Japan, such structural improvement has been called *hoshin kanri*, a system that began during the years 1960 to 1965, as statistical quality control (SQC) transformed into total quality control (TQC).

Because these developments came about as an accumulation of industrial experience, however, no formal systematization existed until recently. For example, there were few books on the subject, with the exception of Professor Y. Nayatani's *Policy Control for TQC Promotion* (1978). To remedy the situation, the Japan Standards Association in December 1986 published a special issue of their magazine, *Standardization and QC*, devoted to *hoshin kanri*. K. Koura, T. Nomi, and I published an article in that issue entitled *"Hoshin Kanri as a Part of TQC"* that became the impetus for this book.

We have tried to explain *hoshin kanri* by giving practical examples illustrating its principles and offering certain points of caution. In Chapter 1 I summarize areas such as the role of *hoshin kanri* in TQM promotion. In Chapter 2 Mr. Nomi explains each step of the process of implementing *hoshin kanri*, organizing his discussion to correspond with the various cases given later in the book. In Chapters 3 and 4 Mr. Koura offers specific cautions regarding implementation and the relationship of *hoshin kanri* with other control activities. Chapter 5 presents case studies of specific implementation efforts at Aisin-Takaoka, Toppan Printing, Hokuriku-Kogyo, and Kobayashi Kosei. Chapter 6 is the article from the above-mentioned special issue of *Standardization and QC*. Our discussions of some of the problems recently encountered by companies implementing *hoshin kanri* may be of particular help to readers. This book is more a compilation of examples than it is a system manual. For that reason, any company establishing a *hoshin kanri* system should refer to the case studies in Chapter 5 to create a system that is tailored to its own conditions.

We hope that this book will make some contribution toward the establishment of TQM in every company. Our thanks go to the people in those companies where case studies were made available and to Mr. Sawada of the Japan Standards Association for his help in editing this book. On behalf of the editors and authors,

Yoji Akao

Contributors

Chairman of Author Committee:

Y. Akao
Professor
Tamagawa University

Editorial Committee Members:

T. Imai
TQC Promotion Office
Hokuriku-Kogyo Co.

K. Koura
Instructor
Saitama University

Y. Noda
Production Center
Kobayashi Kosei

T. Nomi
Japan Standards Association

A. Ohta
Production Control Department
Aisin-Takaoka Co.

S. Tamura
TQC Promotion Office
Toppan Printing Co.

Understanding *Hoshin Kanri*
An Introduction by Greg Watson

Plans are nothing, planning is everything.
  – Dwight D. Eisenhower

Approaching Business as a System

Much of Japanese quality thinking— if not the fundamental element underlying it — supports putting principle into practice. As this approach to managing is quite appropriate to any situation, its potential impact was recognized early in the Japanese culture. The importance of implementing this concept began sometime before 1645 when Miyamoto Musashi wrote *A Book of Five Rings* as a guide to samurai warriors. The basis of this philosophy was summed up in one word: *heiho*, or *strategy*. The word *heiho* is formed from two Chinese characters: *hei* meaning soldier and *ho* meaning method or form.

In this guide for kendo (or swordsmanship), Musashi said, "If you are thoroughly conversant with strategy, you will recognize the enemy's intentions and have many opportunities to win."[1] Not surprisingly, Japanese business principles, as well as their practices, are often analogous to the art of the samurai warrior. For instance, the seven tools of quality control are modeled after the seven weapons of Benkei, a samurai warrior in the twelfth century.

Similarly, hoshin is related to *heiho* in kendo, Musashi's martial art of sword fighting with the katana. Like *heiho*, the word *hoshin*, is composed of two Chinese characters: *ho* and *shin*; *ho* meaning method or form, and *shin* meaning shiny needle or compass. Taken together the word "hoshin" means a "methodology for strategic direction setting."

Hoshin provides a sound practice for Musashi's principle: "Step by step, walk the thousand mile road."[2]

Managing by a Step-by-Step Process

Hoshin kanri provides a step-by-step planning, implementation, and review process for managed change. Specifically, it is a *systems approach to management of*

---

[1] Miyamoto Musashi, *A Book of Five Rings*, translated by Victor Harris (Woodstock, N.Y.: Overlook Press, 1982), p. 74.
[2] Ibid., p. 66.

change in critical business processes. A system, in this sense, is a set of coordinated processes that accomplish the core objectives of the business.

For every business system there are measures of performance and desired levels of performance. What *hoshin* provides is a planning structure that will bring selected critical business processes up to the desired level of performance. *Hoshin kanri* operates at two levels: First, at what Dr. Joseph Juran called "breakthrough" management or the strategic planning level; and, second, at the daily management level on the more routine or fundamental aspects of the business operation. *Hoshin kanri* has been called the application of Deming's plan-do-check-act to the management process.

The initial considerations in this approach to business system change are as follows:

- Measuring the system as a whole.
- Setting core objectives of the business.
- Understanding the environmental situation in which the business operates.
- Providing resources to perform business objectives.
- Defining processes that constitute the system — their activities, goals, and performance measures and performance feedback adjustments.

Measuring the Whole System

Critical to managing a system is creating a plan that manages the introduction of strategic change initiatives. This is essential because no one should expect to establish a "totally correct" initial direction for any business-system considerations. These business-system considerations include core business objectives, environmental conditions, resource availability, or definitions for all critical business processes.

Hoshin kanri encourages the ability to be adaptive. Since long-range planning is based on information monitored from the business system, the planning process itself must be adaptive and capable of response to changes in the business system. This means that management of the business system must include a regular review or assessment that indicates whether or not the system plan is faltering and must be adjusted or changed. This is achieved through regular reviews of both the planning-implementation progress, as well as the application of the planning methodology itself. Thus, *hoshin* becomes an enabling feature in the continuous improvement of the company's management process, and serves as an information feedback loop that permits continuous responses to the winds of business change.

Setting Core Business Objectives

One premise of hoshin is that people who are charged with executing a plan should participate in the planning process itself. This premise is based on the concept that any plan that incorporates group dialogue will become a stronger plan. An analogy for this approach — which the Japanese call "catchball" — is that people participate in a dialogue in much the same way as a circle of young children play catch with a baseball. We sometimes call this technique "tossing an idea around." The benefit of such activity comes from the fundamental belief that people want to do what they believe is right. Unless they participate in the broader dialogue of the company, they will not know what is right and will tend to suboptimize, or do what is right according to the perspective of their own "egocentric" process. This parochial view of the "best" way to do something — and each of course having his or her own "best" way — is most often not optimal for the overall business system. The objective is to obtain alignment (or consistency) among all participating factions, and focus the business as a coherent whole system on its core objectives. The core objectives become those agreements that can be reached by consensus for the purpose of the business system. In many American businesses this is a process of "management visioning."

Understanding the Environmental Situation

Achieving this goal means that a company's management team must have the ability, desire, and means to communicate, cooperate, and integrate its planning process with the entire business (corporate) structure. *Hoshin kanri* provides this ability by encouraging a dialogue in both the setting of objectives as well as the development of strategies and measures needed to achieve designated business objectives. Hence, the first step in *hoshin*, as is also true in Total Quality Management (TQM), is gaining an understanding of the needs of management's customers.

Satisfying management's customers — which include stockholders, the board of directors, business analysts, and employees, as well as external customers — is central to the *hoshin* method of continuous improvement. The first step toward this is performing an environmental analysis of the situation in which the business system functions. This includes the economic, market, political, technical, social, and legislative aspects of the company's business and how it performs relative to its competitors in these areas. Benchmarking is an important tool for the management team to use in understanding the boundaries of the business system environment.

Benchmarking can be used to help establish the targets used in *hoshin*. What matters most is not how a company is performing relative to its own historical trends, but rather how it is performing in relation to its current competitors. The Malcolm Baldrige National Quality Award (MBNQA) criteria emphasize this fact by seeking competitive information in almost every evaluated category.

Providing Implementation Resources

Hoshin kanri operates on two levels to manage continuous improvement — breakthrough or strategic objectives, and daily management control of the business fundamentals. Daily management (kaizen applied to the business process fundamentals) is the basic control process of a Japanese business, while *hoshin* is used to align and coordinate the business system for specific strategic change initiatives. In general, a company implementing *hoshin* manages no more than three-to-five major strategic change initiatives simultaneously. However, the amount of time dedicated to *hoshin* objectives varies according to job assignment and level within the company. Senior management may spend more than 80 percent of their time on hoshin breakthrough objectives while line employees spend less than 10 percent.

Daily control is part of *hoshin kanri* and cannot be ignored. It represents those "non-strategic changes" or fundamental business processes where change is of a more gradual "kaizen" nature. Therefore, as the objectives cascade down the organization into strategies, it is prudent to track the manpower required for appropriate implementation.

Defining System Processes

Hoshin provides management with an opportunity for *consensus* dialogue about significant system change. A model for this consensus planning and execution process is illustrated below:

Hoshin Model

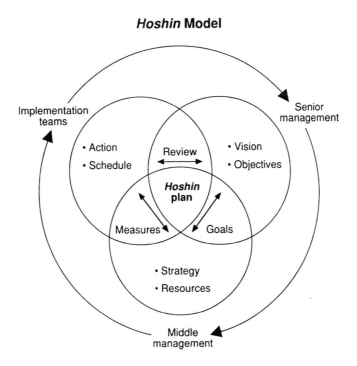

The general movement of the *hoshin kanri* process is from senior management to middle management to the implementation teams. The two-way arrows represent negotiated dialogue or "catchball" used among these three groups to establish and agree on the goals, measures, and review. Senior management is responsible for establishing the "what" of the business system — its vision and core objectives. Middle management negotiates with senior management regarding the goals that indicate completion of the core objectives and is then responsible for developing the "how" of the business system — the strategies for addressing the objectives and the management of the resources to accomplish the plan. Middle management then negotiates with the implementation teams regarding the performance measures that are used to indicate progress toward accomplishing the strategies. The implementation team is then empowered to manage the action and schedule their activities. Senior management then uses a review process to understand both the progress of the implementation teams and the success of their planning system.

The review phase represents what is called in Japan the "Presidential Audit," a quality management review by the senior management team. (This is one potential internal company application of the MBNQA assessment criteria.) It involves letting senior management observe firsthand the detail of the quality system implementation.

This model is a simplification of the methodology presented by Dr. Yoji Akao and his colleagues in this book. They present us with a unique insight into the Japanese method of applying *hoshin kanri*. Their approach provides an important understanding for senior Western managers, since this methodology forms the cornerstone of the Japanese management system.

Understanding Japanese *Hoshin*

Dr. Akao and his fellow authors have presented a wonderful book of fundamental knowledge of the Japanese *hoshin kanri* system. It is important to remember that there are many cultural and business distinctions between implementing a *hoshin* system in Japan and in Western countries. The following table presents some of the key concepts for the promotion (implementation) of the Japanese *hoshin kanri* method. These steps are described further in Chapter 2.

> 1. Establish a company motto, quality policy, and promotion plan.
> 2. Devise long-term and medium-term management strategy.
> 3. Collect and analyze the information.
> 4. Plan the target and means.
> 5. Set the control items and prepare a control item list.
> 6. Deploy the policy.
> 7. Deploy the control items.
> 8. Implement the policy plan.
> 9. Check the results of implementation.
> 10. Prepare the status report for implementing *hoshin kanri*.

The first step of this methodology is unusual for a Western company culture. This step does not mean that management should create a catchphrase, rally round the troops, and shout or sing the company slogan. Indeed, the cross-cultural meaning is much more profound. What this first step means is that management needs to take a careful look at their business by conducting an environmental scan. This step in Akao's methodology is not stated strongly enough. The core objective that most businesses use is the "vision" of the management team, complemented by an understanding of the competitive situation, and joined together with the technological environment and resulting market opportunities available from the current situation. The following process helps to understand how a company would conduct such an analysis of its environmental situation in preparation for *hoshin kanri*:

1. Assessing the need for change.
2. Evaluating the business environmental situation (i.e., political, economic, social, techonological, and cultural).
3. Understanding competitive trends by benchmarking, conducting industry analysis, and evaluating competitive intelligence.
4. Projecting trend information to develop alternative future scenarios.
5. Building mutual consensus among the management team on implications of observed and projected indicators.
6. Developing business objectives that address possible alternatives.
7. Identifying core objectives and gaining shared commitment within the business.

Beginning with the establishment of a company's business vision and its core business objectives, *hoshin kanri* focuses on making competitive change — the change required to gain or maintain market position. The core objectives thus reflect the underlying business purpose of the organization. As soon as an industry leader establishes the long-term market advantage of superior performance based on a particular performance indicator, then the rest of that industry will be at a competitive disadvantage. In summation, a successful corporate strategy typically begins with a realistic assessment of the current environmental situation, a coherent vision of the future, and the understanding of the transition required to bridge from the present to the future. *Hoshin* helps to sustain competitive advantage by providing a structure for linking the core objectives into the current competitive situation.

Observing the Benefits of *Hoshin*

Hoshin has been adapted to several major American companies, including Hewlett-Packard, Florida Power & Light, Procter and Gamble, Intel, and Xerox. These companies have recognized the advantages of *hoshin* over other planning systems. *Hoshin* is the application of plan-do-check-act to business process management. Comparing the Malcolm Baldrige National Quality Award evaluation method to *hoshin* results in an interesting observation: they are parallel planning and execution methodologies. While the Baldrige evaluates companies on their approach and deployment of quality throughout the company and observes the results from implementing the quality approach, *hoshin* provides a method for developing a companywide approach and deploying it for results. The advantages most often cited focus on the communication improvement from a documented, open planning, implementation, and review system. Specific advantages include:

- Everyone knows how his or her work relates to the strategic (*hoshin*) and tactical (daily management) operation of the business system.
- Linked core objectives and implementation strategies clarify the communication among cross-functional activities and improve the buy-in among diverse business activities.
- Review of progress is structured to permit open discussion of the unfolding application of management's core objectives for business-system improvement.
- *Hoshin kanri* methodology is continuously reviewed to improve the operational planning system of the business rather than to leave an unquestioned, static, financially focused system in place.

Applying *Hoshin* Methods

Many of the American companies that have implemented *hoshin kanri* have shared their implementation methods in the public domain. The methods of Hewlett-Packard, Florida Power & Light, and Xerox have been combined into the following "idealized" *hoshin* system. This example consists of four related forms that help to manage the *hoshin* system implementation. These forms do not reflect accurately what any particular company uses in its current implementation, but were developed to provide a nonprescriptive "best practices" integration of the principles of *hoshin*. The purpose of presenting these four forms is to provide a more concrete example of the practice of *hoshin*.

1. Hoshin *Plan Summary*

A *hoshin* plan summary is used to present an overview of the entire *hoshin* plan. This form provides specific details for each core objective and complements the individual *hoshin* action plans for each objective. Some of the key features of this form include:

- Statement of core objectives with their associated owners, short-term and long-term goals, and their supporting implementation strategies with their targets and milestones.
- A matrix that describes the relationship between each of the *hoshin* implementation strategies and the company's Total Quality Management focus (the sample form indicates four key TQM focuses for continuous improvement — quality, cost, cycle time, and safety).

Hoshin Plan Summary

Core Objectives	Management Owner	Goals		Implementation Strategies	Target		Improvement Focus			
		Short term	Long term		Short term	Long term	Quality	Cost	Cycle time	Safety

 Symbol indicates a strong relationship between improvement focus and a specific strategy

2. Hoshin *Action Plan*

Once the overall *hoshin kanri* approach for a company has been developed, it needs to be deployed. The first form used in this deployment process is a *hoshin* action plan. The action plan is used to record the detailed information that links a particular core objective to the implementation strategies. Some of the key features of this form include:

- Recording of specific administrative information regarding both the ownership of the core objective as well as its review status and progress against the goals and performance targets.
- Summary of the environmental situation that lead to the assessment of this particular objective being considered to be a core objective to the business system.
- Statement of the core objective.
- Recording of the agreed-upon short-term and long-term goals for the core objective.
- Description of the strategies that will be pursued for implementation of the core objective, identification of the strategy owners and the performance targets and schedule milestones that have been agreed upon for each strategy.

3. Hoshin *Implementation Plan*

The *hoshin* implementation plan is the document used for recording progress in the execution of the strategy. It includes a listing of implementation activities required to reach closure on the strategy and the current status of schedule milestones and performance results as compared to the initial projections. This Gantt chart format is typical of most *hoshin* implementation plans. By adding the actual schedule to the original schedule and actual performance to the target performance, this form supplements the hoshin implementation review form.

4. Hoshin *Implementation Review*

The *hoshin* implementation review form is used to record progress in the performance measure that represents the target for this strategy of the core objective. As indicated in the example, this form is one place where the company's performance relative to industry average and world-class benchmarks should be recorded. An additional feature of this form is the listing of the current status of the highest priority implementation issues, and the individual owner who is working to resolve each issue by the targeted resolution date.

Hoshin Action Plan

Hoshin Objective Title:

Department/Location:

Review Team:

Management Owner:

Date:

Next Review:

Environmental Situation Summary:

Core Objective:

Strategy (Owner)

Targets and Milestones

Goals

Short term:

Long term:

Hoshin Implementation Plan

Hoshin Objective Title:

Strategy Number:

Strategy Owner:

Date Updated:

Next Review:

Strategy Statement	Implementation Activities	Activity Owner	Schedule and Milestones (Plan vs. Actual)							Performance	
			MMYR	MMYR	MMYR	MMYR	MMYR	MMYR	MMYR	Target	Actual

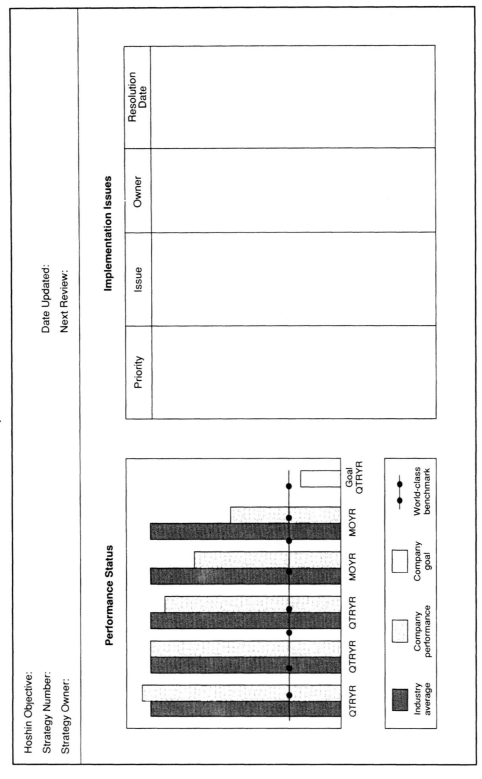

Closing Comment

Dr. Akao has done the professional quality community a great service by providing this gem. It is still a rough-cut stone from the perspective of a Western reader; however, it does provide valuable insights into some of the lessons learned by our Japanese counterparts. As with any quality principle being considered for practical application, we must consider the still sound advice of Dr. Deming and adapt those *hoshin kanri* principles that apply to our own particular business environment and not blindly adopt the *hoshin kanri* method. Benchmarking our current planning process against this Japanese methodology is a good place to start for developing an understanding of the performance gap that can be closed by using the *hoshin kanri* methods.

*   *   *   *   *   *   *   *   *   *   *   *   *   *   *   *   *   *   *

Gregory H. Watson is presently a business advisor for major corporations in Europe, Latin America, and North America. He is a Director-at-Large of the American Society for Quality Control and a Certified Quality Engineer. He has served on the Board of Examiners for the Malcolm Baldrige National Quality Award, Texas Quality Award, New York State Excelsior Award, New Jersey Quality Achievement Award, and the American Productivity & Quality Center Benchmarking Award.

Greg has held executive positions as a quality officer at both Xerox Corporation and Compaq Computer Corporation. He was Manager of Quality Leadership Development at the Hewlett-Packard Company during the time that *hoshin kanri* was introduced. In addition to working on his organization's planning process as a divisional planning manager, Greg was a member of the development team for *hoshin* training. Greg has written several quality-related books: *The Benchmarking Workbook* (Productivity Press, 1992), *Strategic Benchmarking* (John Wiley & Sons, 1993), and *Business Systems Engineering* (John Wiley & Sons, 1994).

CHAPTER 1

TQM and *Hoshin Kanri*

Japanese quality control in its present form is based on the statistical quality control (SQC) that was brought over from the United States after World War II. Later in Japan we developed total quality control (TQC), which in other countries has come to be known as CWQC (companywide quality control) or TQM (total quality management).

The transition from SQC to TQC occurred during the years 1961 to 1965 in companies whose achievements in quality earned them the Deming Prize. These companies were Nissan Automotive (1960), Teijin and Nippon Denso (1961), Sumitomo-Denko (1962), Nippon-Kayaku (1963), Komatsu (1964), and Toyota Jiko (1965). During this period the concepts of control items and *hoshin kanri*, or policy deployment, were born.

It was also during these years that the emphasis in industry shifted from chemicals to mechanical assembly of automobiles and home appliances. Because of this, new products were needed in rapid succession, and this required establishing quality standards throughout the entire system, beginning with the product planning stage. SQC centered on production evolved naturally into TQC.

The official introduction of TQC to Japan was a one-year series of TQC seminars held in 1960 for *SQC* magazine. Dr. Feigenbaum, who led those seminars, defined TQC as an effective system for integrating the development of quality among various parts of a company, quality retention and quality improvement for economical production, and service that considers its goal to be complete satisfaction of consumers.

This definition of TQC does not allow for the involvement of staff, management, and other workers, and until recently, such involvement was indeed absent, at least in the United States. However, the Japan Standards Association and the Union of Japanese Scientists and Engineers (JUSE) have held seminars for various levels in the organization — including top management, department and section heads, staff, supervisors, and QC circle leaders — so that in companies where TQC has been introduced in this country, it is deployed as a means of securing quality accountability at each of these levels. Thus, a CWQC peculiar to Japan has evolved.

Hoshin kanri, also known as *hoshin planning* or *management by policy* or (as we will refer to it here) *policy deployment*, has its origins in SQC. In 1958 the following audit items were introduced into the Deming Prize: policy and plan, organization, interdepartmental relationships, standardization, analysis, control, and effects. Applications submitted for prize examination were therefore required to contain descriptions of TQC promotion policy or company policy. This was an important factor in emphasizing policy in quality control.

The present-day significance of *hoshin kanri* is exemplified by Komatsu's control point setting chart and Nokawa Shoji's flag method. Nokawa's method, based on the control item list of Teijin Company in 1961 and the concepts of control items and inspection items practiced at Nippon-Kayaku, offered a specific method for target deployment. The "integrated control system chart" (N. Kitahata, 1964) contains information useful to many issues still being discussed today. The term *hoshin kanri* was not used at that time but the same control system we use today was in action then.

Hoshin kanri is just one of the pillars of TQM.* Others, such as production control and cost control, are in operation daily in every company. These daily controls are the basis of business management. To survive within the dynamic environments of social, economic, and technological change, however, a company must use strategic management to respond to competitive situations. Maintaining the status quo amounts to regression, so companies must develop. To do this, they need to clarify both the apparent and the intangible weaknesses of their systems so that these weaknesses are eliminated and the overall systems improved. This is what makes policy deployment so important: It clarifies specific annual target policies derived from the long- and medium-term policies that encompass the long-term visions of the company. It strives to achieve targets through action plans intended to improve the control system. These action plans are then deployed for their targets and their policies. Meanwhile, actions such as Quality Assurance (QA) need to be in permanent motion since they involve daily activities more than does policy deployment. Daily activity is the basis of policy deployment, which improves the level of the QA activities as Feigenbaum defined them; but such companywide improvement activities at all levels of an organization are just one feature of TQM.

Hoshin Kanri and Target Control

Target control was proposed by E. C. Schleh (1963) as "management by results" and is based on scientific action. The concept originated in social psychology and emphasizes motivating people to achieve targeted goals. Under its volunteer approach, workers set up purposes and work toward their achievement.

---

* In the United States TQM is equivalent to Japanese TQC. With the author's permission we have changed the term TQC to TQM for clarity in communicating the principles of a company-wide quality approach in which the implementation of hoshin kanri is central.

When the concept of target control was introduced to the Japanese in 1963, it immediately appealed to management. Because it could be implemented easily, it soon grew popular in Japan. Target control emphasizes results, but today the process that produces these results must also be analyzed. Thus, TQM looks for the process that produces bad results. Bad results come about because of certain factors. You could define the process that produces bad results as a conglomeration of many factors. In TQM you look for the true factors. You collect data so that any action you take is based on facts rather than on ideology. The data must be analyzed so that the factors are grasped scientifically and can thus be eliminated as obstructions to the achievement of desired results. That is why methods such as statistical analysis are still in use today.

For *hoshin kanri* in TQM, the plan-do-check-action (PDCA) cycle is the most important item of control. In this cycle you make a plan that is based on policy *(plan)*; you take action accordingly *(do)*; you check the results *(check)*; and if the plan is not fulfilled, you analyze the cause and take further action by going back to the plan *(action)*.

The PDCA cycle is important in setting up the policy itself, as well. The variance between the plan and the actual situation is evaluated each business term or annually, and the cause of such variance analyzed, with the results incorporated into next year's policy. Here you do not look at the value of the results but at the variance between the plan and the actual situation. If the cause is not clarified, then the same discrepancy could appear in the next period as well. The process that produced the bad results obviously has some weaknesses, and these need to be discovered and eliminated. You emphasize the process rather than the results and improve the process to achieve better results. This approach, *hoshin kanri* or policy deployment, is distinctly different from Schleh's target control, although in the early days of TQC the two terms were often used interchangeably.

Target and Policy

Target can be defined as "expected results." *Means* can be defined as "guidelines for achieving a target." The means show how to achieve the target, in other words.

Generally, *policy* is used in the broadest sense, so that a target and means combined can be called a policy. If the means show the direction, then you clarify the specific steps for achieving the target by basing them on these means. Then you can determine an action plan with a timetable.

"Reduction in rejection rate" is neither an implementation item nor a means. It is a target. *How* to reduce the rejection rate is important, however, and the specifics related to them are action items. To improve on expected results you must discover weaknesses in the processes that produce these rejects. Means show the way to discover and eliminate those weaknesses. Examples of means are "thorough process analysis" or "promotion of standardization." Specific corrective actions will emerge after data based on such means have been analyzed.

An action plan for improvement should not be bogged down in detail. Plans will become increasingly detailed with each year-end analysis of variance. However, since plans are usually set on timetables of six months or a year, they tend to be broadly stated as well. You may need to add an action plan chart for additional implementation items as the improvements progress.

Target Deployment

The best method for target deployment currently is the flag* method (Figure 1-1). It combines a Pareto analysis chart and a fishbone diagram.

First, Pareto analysis is made for the section's rejection rate (upper left). The department head establishes a target for reducing rejections and then meets with section heads to set up section targets. Here, a major improvement is added to the major rejection item. Exercise caution here. An across-the-board reduction of 5 percent, for example, fails to address priorities, while a 3 percent reduction in an already-low rejection rate is nonsense. In the latter case, you should shoot for zero or for maintaining the current percentage.

Next, you make a Pareto deployment for each group and establish targets for group leaders. This corresponds to target deployment in a normal organization. Pareto deployment for each product based on a control graph of the department head becomes the target deployment for the project team representing each product. In a nonstandard organization, a Pareto deployment and the resulting target per phenomenon at the section or group can become a target for deployment for the QC team (shown by the dotted frames in Figure 1-1). Members that are necessary are called in to these teams, crossing the boundaries of departments in order to analyze the corrective actions, make standards, and prevent repetition. Then the team is dissolved.

---

* The flag method, developed by Komatsu in 1965, aligns means (managers' critical actions or policies) with targets (the primary directions of the organization), and measures numerical results monthly. (See Bob King, *Hoshin Planning, The Developmental Approach*, Methuen, MA: GOAL/QPC, 1989, Chapter 6.)

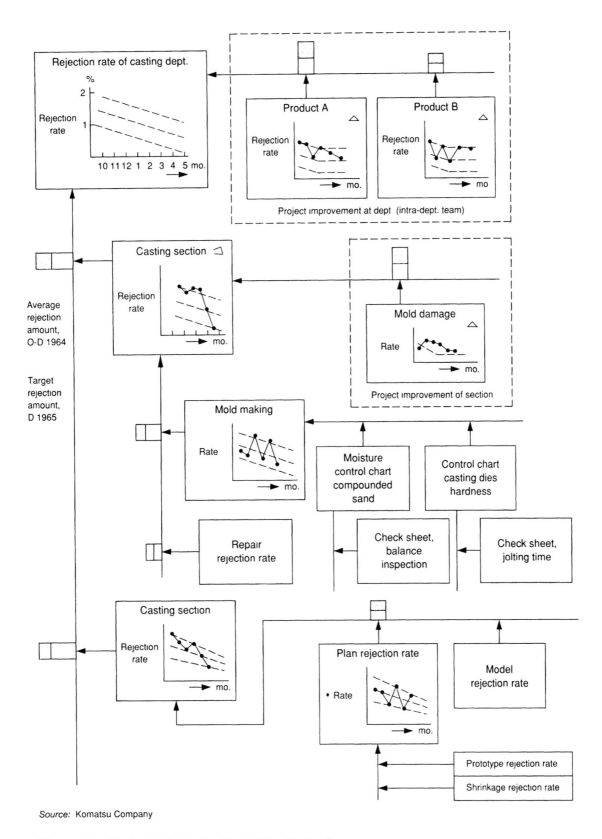

Source: Komatsu Company

Figure 1-1. Control Point Setup Chart (Flag Method)

Means Deployment

The same type of deployment used for targets can also be used for means. For example, to raise the level of QA actions, you need to address the following items:

- Enhance process control
- Improve the process
- Control through use of enhanced inspection and control charts
- Control through promotion of quality and improvement of process deployment capability

This deployment method can be applied to the action plan of a department or section, a plan based on the action items relevant to that department or section at each stage and adapted to their time schedules.

Hoshin kanri is centered on an action plan and carried out through deployment of means. It tends to become a formal control oriented to methods, which means that even though the form of the system is well arranged, the desired results might remain elusive. Thus, the pursuit of an ideal form for its own sake could leave weaknesses undiscovered. A thorough analysis of system weakness based on a thorough check of operations (without overdependence on function deployment) is necessary.

Deployment of means is performed only after criteria for evaluating the plan's results have been established. This may be a difficult task when undertaken jointly by departments that are indirectly related, although it is important to an objective understanding of the matter at hand. Other difficulties arise in sustaining an effort for a long time or in trying to use numbers to evaluate the rate of achievement.

Target Deployment and Means Deployment

When target deployment and means deployment are performed separately, without regard to the other, they each become deficient. The former emphasizes only the results, possibly missing the real cause, while the latter tends to become a formal control focused on methods. *Hoshin kanri* combines the two methods so that policy reflects both target and means. Generally, the means are necessary to achieve the target and in order to be improved may become the target of the next stage, thus themselves needing means by which to be achieved. Linking the means and the target is the only way to deploy both. The flag method does not show means but does indicate detailed targets. The purpose by itself is a linking system, as are the means. However, the means derived from policy and means based on each stage of the target deployment will not necessarily be the same. That is why it is difficult to express target and means in one dimension. Thus, you generally use a matrix (two-dimensional chart) to show the correlation between these heterogeneous subjects. Especially effective is the *target-means relation matrix chart*, which combines target deployment charts and means deployment charts (Figure 1-2).

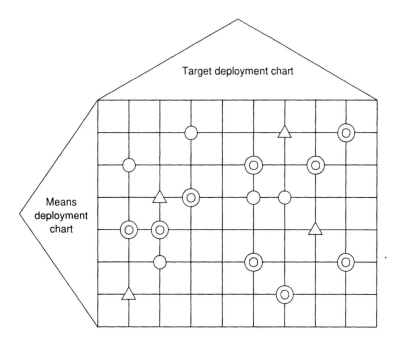

Figure 1-2. Target-Means Relationship Matrix Chart (Conceptual Chart)

Means deployment and target deployment can be performed independently and then later combined. The target and means of the department head should be clarified before any action is taken, however. That way, quality, amount, and cost will be shown, facilitating overall deployment by the departmental staff. (At this stage, neither the target amount nor the tentative value is given.)

With the target deployment chart in hand, the department head and the head of the business department play "catchball"* to determine target values and the

---

* *Catchball* refers to the reiterative up, down, and horizontal communications necessary for effective determination of target and means.

means to achieve them, decisions that are based on the policy of the business department. At the same time, they set action items for the department head. Next, the department head creates a target-means matrix and checks out the adequacy of its deployment. On the means deployment chart, primary-, secondary-, and tertiary means become policies for the business department, department head, and departmental action items, respectively. This matrix allows you to determine whether improvements are adequate in achieving the targets, or breaks in the status quo. If they are not, then you make adjustments.

Not every aim (purpose) of a company can be quantified. However, items that are important but are not shown as target deployment items must be added as purpose deployment items, even though they cannot be quantified. In this matrix the symbols *(o)*, *O*, and Δ indicate target items that strongly effect improvement, have some effect, or have a limited effect, respectively.

Action items marked with an (o) indicate control items that need to be checked. Monitor the progress of those whose characteristic value is difficult to determine. Also, consult the target deployment chart in order to keep progress on course. Preparing a matrix is very helpful when planning policy. The final policy paper does not have to be in a matrix form, but rather in any form that is convenient. Deploying a matrix chart from the top to the bottom is best done as shown in Figure 1-3, after a system chart is prepared for each target and plan. An implementation chart, like that shown in Figure 1-4, can also be used.

Hoshin Kanri and Control Items

The focus of policy deployment on a plan has given rise to problems in its implementation. The plan orientation control items (control characteristics) to be established for each action item in the action plan.

For example, at one company, when a check was made on the control characteristics of each action item, everything looked good. However, when important management control characteristics such as profit, rejection loss, customer claim, and delivery were checked by the target-means matrix (Figure 1-2), these action items were found to be irrelevant. To prevent such an occurrence, you need to apply the PDCA cycle to each control characteristic for each action item, whether or not the action item was performed. If any action item is found to have no effect on the rate of achievement, it should be eliminated. An exception would be in the case of the development department, where the rate of progress can be used to

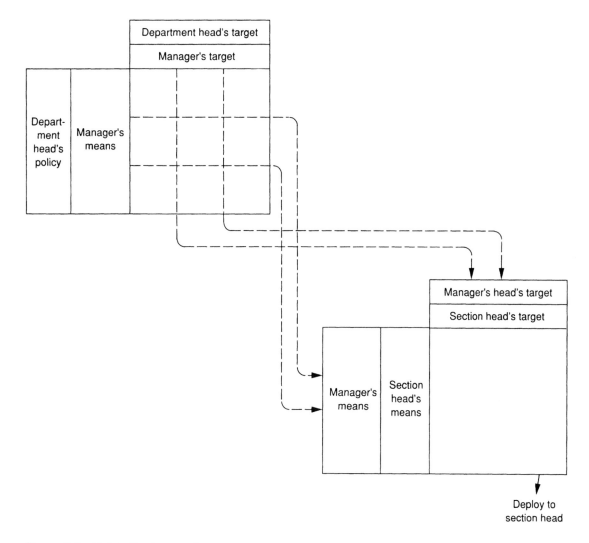

Figure 1-3. Matrix Deployment

gauge the value of the development process; this could be a single control characteristic, depending on the purpose for which it is used.

The target-means matrix allows you to determine whether the means to achieve the purpose or target is there or not. Its effectiveness depends on the extent to which you have studied any inhibiting causes for the factor system (process), using variance analysis on the actual performance of the previous term or year. If the implementation plan cannot be graphically shown, then any action taken in accordance with the plan cannot produce the desired result. Thus, thorough measurement of actual results is crucial.

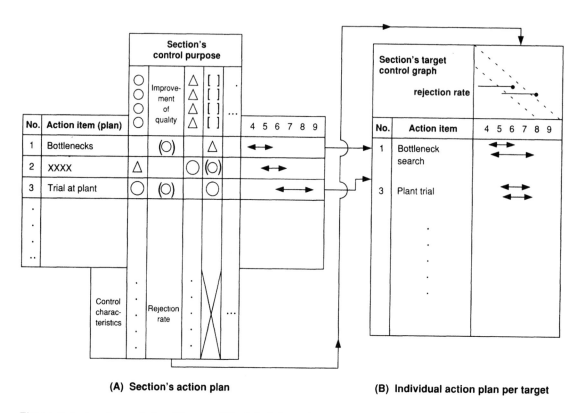

(A) Section's action plan   (B) Individual action plan per target

Figure 1-4. Implementation Plan and Its Administration

The action items in part A of Figure 1-4 show the results of a check on progress. The PDCA cycle should be used with a control graph, such as that shown in part B of Figure 1-4. This clarifies the result characteristics, or expected results. Thus, when unexpected results are obtained during any monthly progress check, you immediately take action on that variance. If the initial target is not achieved even though the plan is being adhered to, then an analysis of inhibiting factors in the process must be performed again. If a new factor is pulled out, corrective action for it is either taken immediately or added to the action items. This is the PDCA control action through use of a control graph.

You cannot necessarily achieve targets by following the implementation items planned at the beginning of the business year or business term. You must also continue to perform factor analysis on processes and to seek proper means by which to achieve the target. Items that are addressed by performance of the job or process are called *control items* or *control characteristics*. The concept of control items and inspection items was proposed in 1964. Unfortunately, these terms have been defined in various ways, creating confusion about the concept. The important ideas behind them, described by K. Ishikawa (1962), are *check with results* and *check with cause*, a distinction common in Japanese QC.

Because *control item* has various meanings, it is usually a generic term. However, the general, broad definition and classification of synonyms in Table 1-1 may be used.

Table 1-1. Control Item Terminology

Control item	Broadly defined	Narrowly defined	
Checked with results (targets)	Control characteristic Control item	Control item	Control point
Checked with cause (means, factors)	Evaluation characteristic Control point	Inspection item	Checkpoint Inspection point

Strictly speaking, a control point and a control item can be distinguished by their relative position and the time at which the former takes over from the latter. However, this distinction is difficult to fathom and offers no significant merit. It seems more practical to understand the two terms as synonyms. For example, a control item in the broad sense can be understood as a control item of cause and a control point in the broad sense can be understood as a control item of results. The concepts for control items are discussed further in Chapter 3, and additional references can be found in the Bibliography.

Hoshin Kanri and QC Circles

A brief review of the concept and principles of QC circles can advance an understanding of policy deployment. QC circle activities are based on the ideas of *autonomous control* and the performance of improvement activities in the *work area*. Policy deployment refers to activities by *managers*. The two concepts must be clearly distinguished.

Deploying a target in the flag system for assignment to QC circle activities is not appropriate from the perspective of the QC circle. Normally, everyone — from managers to group leaders — establishes their own targets and means, which are based on their own responsibilities and achieved through joint effort with their staff and subordinates. Members of the QC circle, of course, bear one part of this responsibility.

QC circle activities are undertaken to clarify and correct problems on the work floor; the problems, or activity themes, are chosen voluntarily by circle members. If the problems of circles are also the problems of management, then ideally they should correspond with the targets and means of the group heads.

Thus, section and group leaders should clarify critical problems for QC circles when establishing target and means. A common understanding of both is essential to policy deployment. Despite the voluntary nature of QC circle activities, coordination of circle themes with management's policies is to everyone's benefit. It promotes satisfaction among circle members, supports the policies of section and group leaders, and enhances the performance of the company.

CHAPTER 2

Promotion of *Hoshin Kanri*

Born as a part of TQM, *hoshin kanri* is a system for quality control and continuous improvement activities. It has been given various definitions, the simplest of which are listed in Table 2-1.

Table 2-1. Definitions of *Hoshin Kanri*

November 1984	K. Nayatani, *Way of Looking and Thinking of Things* (JUSE): *Hoshin kanri* is a systematic control activity for the achievement of annual management policy (president's policy) based on a company motto, management concepts, long/medium-term plans, etc., on which all job levels perform PDCA for harmonizing each policy.
November 1984	S. Mizuno, *Companywide Overall QC* (Nikka-Giren): *Hoshin kanri* is to improve performance continuously by disseminating and deploying the direction, targets, and plans of company management to top management and all employees so that all job levels can act on the plans, evaluate, study, and feedback results while continually performing PDCA. The purpose of *hoshin kanri* is to break away from the status quo and make a great leap up by analyzing current problems and deploying in response to environmental conditions.
January 1985	S. Miura, ed., *TQC Terminology Dictionary* (Japan Standards Association): *Hoshin kanri:* All activity within an organization for systematic achievement of medium/long-term management plan or annual management policy, which is established as the means for achievement of management purpose. Often, it is used for annual management policy.
March 1986	T. Sugimoti, ed., *QC of Clerical-Sales Service Work* (Nippon Kikaku Kyokai): Briefly, *hoshin kanri* is a system for effective achievement of target (Q, C, D, often) by banding all capabilities of the total organization of a company.
1987	Summary Definition *Hoshin kanri* is, for the achievement of management's purpose, a system of • enhancement of the company's overall capability and banding together all capability of the company for improvement of performance, through: • deployment of a unified policy and plan (implementation, check, action for improvement) established as an annual management plan based on a company motto (basic company management concept). Management strategy is a form of long/medium-term management plan annual management plan, by: • utilizing major resources for management (people, goods, money) and optimally bonding together quality, volume, cost, and timing (delivery). (Use of QC concepts and methods in the above-mentioned processes is necessary.)

Overall Control System

Central to any discussion of *hoshin kanri* and its role in TQM is the overall control system that is at its foundation. Overall control systems were created to improve companywide performance through promotion of structural improvements. This so-called management revolution developed in response to the rapid changes that many Japanese companies faced in the 1960s.

Nippon-Kayaku, which received the Deming Prize for achievement in quality in 1963, was the first to publish an overall control system. Two examples that were published later are given in Figures 2-1 and 2-2. Figure 2-2, from Komatsu Company, shows details of the flag method described in Chapter 1.

Hoshin Kanri: Basic Concept

Hoshin kanri (policy deployment) is the means by which both the overall control system and TQM are deployed. The ultimate purpose of implementing policy deployment is to create companywide QA, which is based on the philosophy that *quality is supreme* and which takes a *market-in* (customer-oriented) approach. Policy deployment is a system of management to implement QA, which is often considered to be the core of TQM.

The *hoshin kanri* system can be shown on a chart, usually arranged as a matrix. Figure 2-3 is a summary of the hoshin chart concept. A simpler approach is the concept chart of Kobayashi Kosei (Figure 2-4).

As stated earlier, policy deployment is a means of promoting companywide quality control and continuous improvement. Important to this system are the PDCA control method, needed for maintenance items, and a concept that emphasizes improvement, particularly QC solutions to critical problems. The clarification of critical problems is necessary, in fact, at both ends of the policy deployment process, as is shown in Figure 2-3.

Implementation of the overall control system and the *hoshin kanri* system in Figure 2-3 must occur on a companywide scale while also addressing department, operations, and if possible, section levels.

Hoshin Kanri as a Part of TQM

Policy deployment as a part of TQM should be distinguished from annual policy and plan making by its embrace of long- and medium-term management

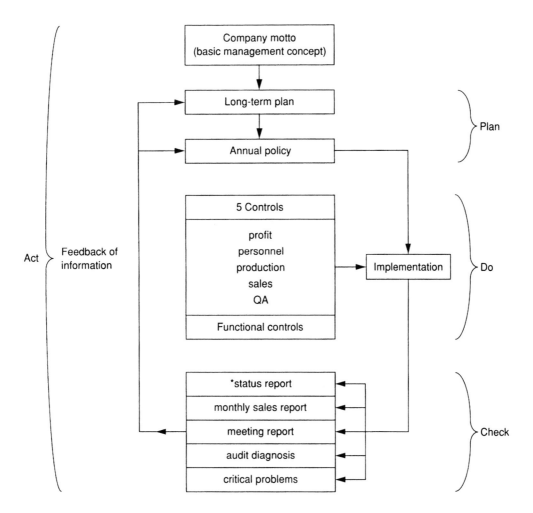

Act } Feedback of information

* Abbreviation of *hoshin kanri* implementation status report

Figure 2-1. Overall Control System at Bridgestone Tire Company (Awarded 1968)

plans, which are the foundation of an annual policy and plan. Moreover, policy deployment is not the same as QC. Rather, it uses the concepts and methods of QC to solve problems in its role as a part of TQM.

Basic Promotion of *Hoshin Kanri*

Many terms are used to explain the basic promotion methods — for example, management plan and policy plan — but the distinction among them is not uniformly understood. The terms used in this book are standard in TQM, particularly

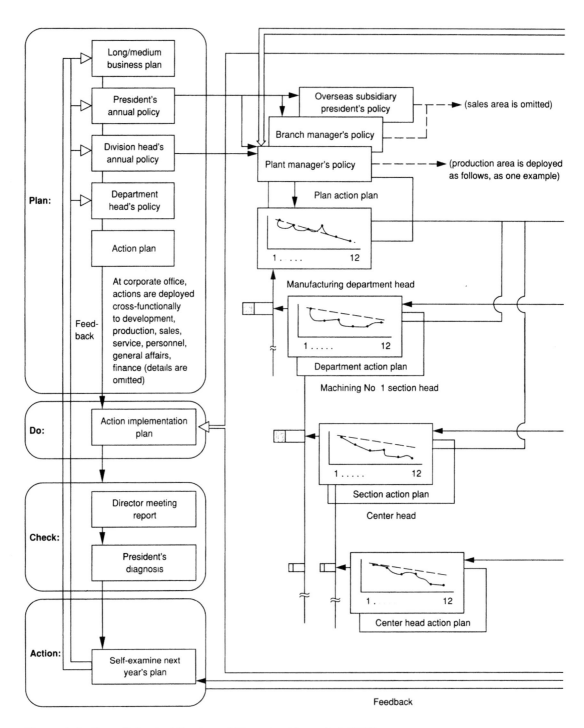

Figure 2-2. Overall Control System at Komatsu (Awarded 1964)

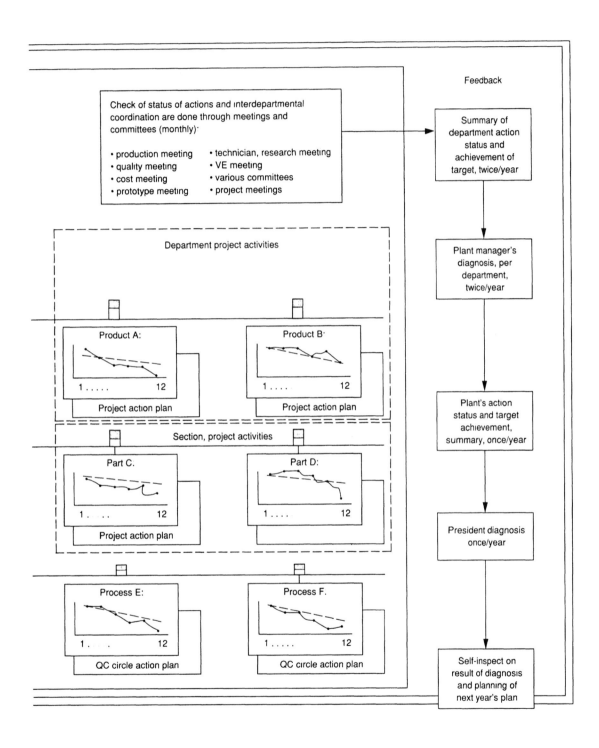

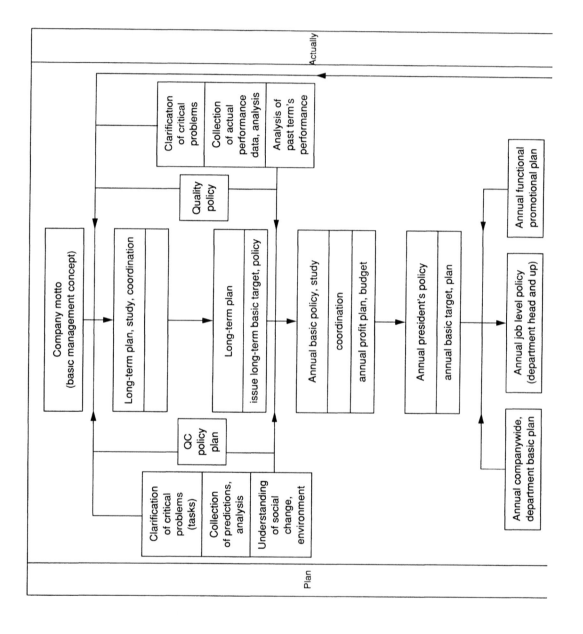

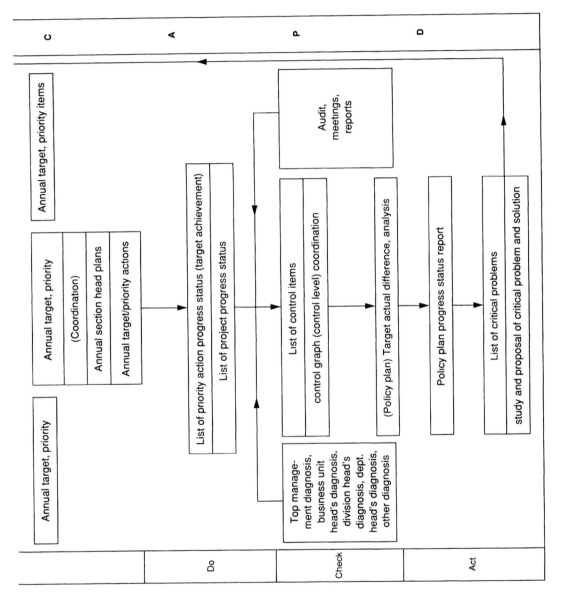

Figure 2-3. *Hoshin Kanri* : **Basic Concept**

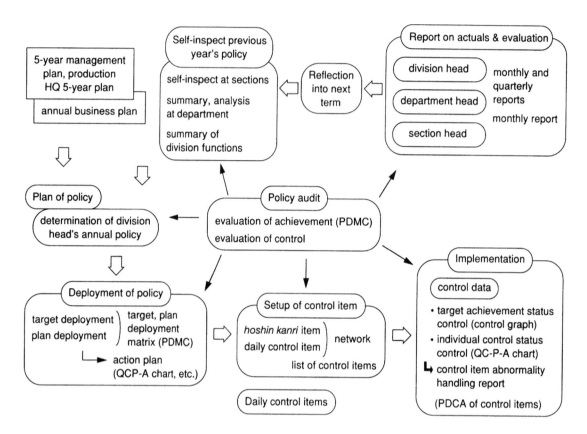

Figure 2-4. *Hoshin Kanri* at Kobayashi Kosei

in policy deployment. The following ten steps outline the process of policy deployment promotion.

1. Establish a company motto, quality policy, and promotion plan
2. Devise long- and medium-term management strategies
3. Collect and analyze the information
4. Plan the target and means
5. Set control items and prepare a control item list
6. Deploy the policy
7. Deploy the control items
8. Implement the policy plan
9. Check the results of implementation
10. Prepare the status report for implementing *hoshin kanri*

Step 1: Establish a Company Motto, Quality Policy, and Promotion Plan

Policy deployment begins when managers establish a company motto, purpose, mission, or management vision. Supporting this basic concept are a quality policy and a policy for the promotion of QC. The clarification of a management concept is essential to quality policy and QC promotion plans and to successful implementation of policy deployment (Kayano, 1955).

As shown in Table 2-2, the company vision or purpose is expressed as a general guideline. Use of a system chart or matrix chart is an effective means of applying quality deployment methods to departments, sections, or quality, cost, and delivery (QCD) functions. Thus, a company motto (or management concept) is expressed in general terms and then broken down into the specifics of a quality policy and QC promotion plan.

Table 2-2. Company Motto, Management Concept, and Quality Policy (Simple Form)

Company Motto   • Contribute to society through highest quality. (Bridgestone) [1]
Management Concept   • Achieve customer satisfaction, employee happiness, and company's expansion by making quality supreme. (Hoyo-Seiki) [2]
Quality Policy   • Customer satisfaction is sought through the philosophy that quality is supreme. (Comany) [3]   • Understand customers' needs and solve problems. This must be TI's product and service. Let's do correct work from the start. It must be the norm for all of TI's employees. (Nippon T.I. Bipolar Division) [4]
QC Policy   This company offers a quality product, good service, low fees, a stable supply, and safe operating conditions so as to respond to customers' needs in a positive manner. (Kansai-Electric) [5]
[1] Deming Award 1968 (implementation)   [2] Deming Award 1985 (implementation, small industry)   [3] Deming Award 1985 (implementation, small industry)   [4] Deming Award 1985 (division)   [5] Deming Award 1985 (implementation)

Point of Caution in Step 1

A policy deployment program that lacks policies for quality and for QC promotion will also lack a central point (core point). It will run the risk of becoming separated from QC.

Further information on the various terms just discussed can be found in the following sources:

1. *Hoshin kanri*
   - Y. Noya (1982)
   - K. Nayatani (1978)
   - S. Mochimoto (1985)

2. Policy for QC promotion
   - K. Nayatani (1978)
   - K. Ishihara (1984)

3. Quality policy
   - K. Ishihara (1984)
   - S. Mizuno (1984)

4. Quality deployment
   - S. Mizuno and Y. Akao (1978)

Step 2: Devise Long- and Medium-term Management Strategies

Cultivate a strategy of quick response to changes (emphasizing sales strategies based on market-in concepts) by establishing long- and medium-term plans. These plans should be in line with company goals and priorities. To achieve the long- and medium-term targets, set up a series of strategic priorities based on the collection and analysis of data. Tables 2-3 and 2-4 list major items affecting company environment that might be used as a basis for establishing management strategy. T. Sagimoto (1986) and H. Mori (1986) developed these lists as starting points from which to establish management strategy themes, or tasks.

Long- and medium-term management plans have had to change in Japan in response to the free trade problems of the 1960s, the low-growth problems of the 1970s, and the strong yen problems of the 1980s. For example, strategic management has replaced strategic planning in the creation of long-term plans.

Points of Caution in Step 2

1. Long- or medium-term plans that are merely extensions of past performances and trends are likely to be of no value.
2. Regardless of the seeming validity of the plan, it is important to clarify your expectations for the company, whatever the time frame. These expectations

**Table 2-3. Environmental Changes Affecting
Management Strategy (1)**

Major Item
1. Resources, energy (petroleum)
2. Foreign currency, yen exchange rate, import restriction, trade friction
3. Pollution, destruction of nature
4. Change in industrial structure
5. Low growth
6. Stronger competition
7. Newly industrialized countries (NICs)
8. War power of advanced countries
9. Foods
10. Product liability
11. Humanism
12. International specialization
13. Technological revolution (software, service, system)
14. Change in age-groups

Table 2-4. Environmental Changes Affecting Management Strategy (2)

Major Item
1. World market: trade friction, international specialization, local production, internationalization of people, domestic reductions
2. International market: diversification, two-polarization, affluence, highly informed society, change in distribution channel
3. New market development: new product, market size, QCD, vertical and horizontal expansion of current market, technology transfer (use of present technology)
4. Competition: distinction/niche product, production engineering, balance and synchronization, microfabrication, GT, CAD, CAM, R&D, patent strategy
5. Product liability problems: against users, society
6. Use of advanced technology: R&D, electronics, optotechnology, biotechnology
7. Sytemization: high value-added products, balance between hardware and software, stratification and standardization
8. Higher level schooling and higher age level
9. Pollution: industrial and home life wastes, air pollution, noise, vibration, etc.
10. Others: plant site, energy/resource conservation, international material sourcing

should be the result of thorough analysis of critical problems, current capabilities, and changes outside and inside the company.   .

3. Start by inspecting your own company to discover what problems exist and what should be done now.

The first-year plan of the long- and medium-term management plans serves as a criterion for deployment and control of the annual policy plan. More on the relationship between long- and medium-term plans and annual policy plans will come later in this book.

Step 3: Collect and Analyze the Information

The next step in policy deployment promotion is the collection and analysis of data pertaining to the company's current situation (Table 2-5). Specifically, you need to take the following steps:

1. Analyze the previous year's performance data in order to understand existing problems and clarify tasks.
   • Understand why targets were not achieved.
   • Understand the problems of implementing the process (using charts).
2. Study information (forecast data) about in-house conditions to understand the problems. For example, look at forecasts of new products, new technology, production, sales, people, products, money, quality, quantity, and cost.
3. Study information (forecast data) on the external environment to understand or clarify problems. For example, look at forecast data on international economic changes, domestic changes, and industrial changes.
4. Arrange and stratify the problems discovered above. Weight them (using Pareto analysis, for example), and then isolate the important ones as critical problems.

In analyzing data, perform the following steps:

1. Analyze the factors of each problem (using a fishbone diagram, for example).
2. Weight these factors (through Pareto analysis or some other method), and confirm which critical factors need to be looked at.
3. Repeat steps 1 and 2 with the results analysis sheet of the previous year.

At the heart of policy deployment are quality control and improvement activities. An exception is the use of the PDCA cycle, which is adapted to policy deployment as CAPD. The "check-action" phase of the PDCA cycle precedes the "plan-do" phase in *hoshin kanri*. A CA study sheet is given in Table 2-6. In the Komatsu system, the CA sheet is replaced by a task proposal sheet.

Table 2-5. Collection and Analysis of Information

Classification	Major items	Classification	Major items
Collection of information	1. Trend of industry • International (economics) • Domestic (economics) • Industry (comparison of competitors with own company) • Other information in and out of company 2. Information or strategy, long/medium-term plan (focusing on important tasks requiring this year's handling) 3. Items pointed out by top management's assessment and other assessments (focusing on important tasks requiring this year's handling) 4. Past performance data 5. Items requiring handling based on various meetings and reports (focusing mainly on important tasks requiring this year's handling)	**Analysis of information**	1. Analyze factors of important problems on the left. 2. Do it with the analysis sheet below "previous year's results analysis sheet" or "previous year's *hoshin kanri* results analysis sheet." 3. Determine critical factors to be looked at.

> Use of QC-like concept and method for above work is effective

The process of collecting and analyzing information can be compared with the process of preparing a food recipe. After assembling the ingredients (collecting the information), you prepare them for cooking (analyze the information). Kobayashi Kosei prepares a results analysis sheet (Figure 2-5) and a basic materials summary (Figure 2-6). This company analyzes the policy implementation results from the previous year and then organizes them to clarify the cause-and-effect relationships among the targets, factors, and plans. This assures an accurate and rational planning of the target and means.

Table 2-6. Check-Act Study Chart

C	
Analysis of this term's performance	**Analysis of problems and causes**

C			A				
Causes picked up	**Confirmation of problems**	**Relation line**	**Conceivable correction measures**	**Relation line**	**Expected result**	**Control purpose**	**Supervisor's policy**
A XXXXX	Data analysis		1. XXXXX				
B XXXXX			2. XXXXX				
C XXXXX			3. XXXXX				
D XXXXX			4. XXXXX				
E XXXXX							

Control characteristics

Step 4: Plan the Target and Means

The planning of target and means can be broken down into three major tasks.

1. Using last year's results analysis sheet, determine a policy and plan (target and means). Note: Means are also known as "priority items," "priority implementation items," and "priority action items," depending on the company.
2. Prepare a policy sheet and action plan sheet that list your supervisor's policy, note who will be in charge, lay out a time schedule, and include other pertinent information.

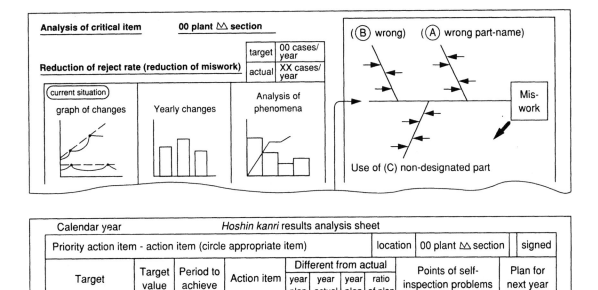

Figure 2-5. Results Analysis Sheet (Kobayashi Kosei)

Year — summary, policy planning basic information						△ △
00 Plant XX section				Date	registration no.	
functional classification	Plan, year —,	Evaluation of actual against plan	Points of self-inspection reports	Audit self-inspection reports	Plan for next year	
Q	1. claim rate of product		1. stratification of claims . . . . 2. mixing of wrong parts	1. result contribution rate of claim analysis . . . . . 2. user's	1. to each claim . . . . 2. claim analysis	
		1. against plan				

Figure 2-6. Basic Information Summary (Kobayashi Kosei)

3. Throughout the process, coordinate with your immediate supervisors and subordinates. Coordination really means discussion, playing catchball, and listening.

As explained in Chapter 1, policy consists of two elements: targets and the means to achieve them. In policy deployment, QC concepts and methods are used to plan target and means.

Komatsu's flag method, already briefly described, is a useful way of setting up and deploying the target. The highlights of this method are given in Figures 2-7, 2-8, and 2-9.

In Komatsu's *hoshin kanri*, the action plan sheets are prepared by each plant manager, branch manager, department head, and section head; at the same time, control items are established. Control points are the control items that are checked with the results (set to achieve or to maintain the initial target) and inspection points or checkpoints the control items that are checked with cause, according to K. Koura (1986). See Figure 2-8, for example.

Procedure	Contents
1. Clarify the job.	problems fed back from action results of last year ⇒ arrange work to be done in this year Set priorities in Pareto manner and classify into quality, quantity, cost, etc.
2. Determine characteristic value to help evaluate degree to which job was completed.	Determine characteristic value in numerical form as a rule for the jobs decided above — — ➤ determination of large flag Select characteristic value of specific target such as "reduce rejects to . . ."
3. Determine which factor is to be controlled for each characteristic value.	Select the factor to be controlled in priority for improvement or maintenance of large flag thus determined. Analyze data on result and find out degree of contribution to characteristic value → summarize into control point setup chart. For the selection of these factors, use a fishbone diagram. Select the manner that best suits each case of control. Break down per in-charge department or per item. rejects at department rejects at group rejects at section

Figure 2-7. Setup (Flag Raising) and Deployment of Control Points (Komatsu)

Procedure	Contents
4. Assign controller.	Using the control point setup chart, assign control points, and determine who controls which flag. • Standardized factors that are stable → control point of subordinates • Control point of subordinates that contributes much to characteristics-value of own → special control point. • Control points to be dealt with by another department → issue problem handling sheet → other department's control point → other department's inspection point (when needed).
5. Fill in target line and handling limit line.	As controllers are assigned, discuss timetable of improvement by factors and fill in ⬚ on Pareto chart and add to each flag a target line and handling limit line.
6. Weave it into action plan sheet.	At the same time, action plans to achieve these targets are woven into action plan sheet. Thus, fishbone diagram and control points are determined from analysis of data.
7. In case of team or staff action:	 In a case other then line activity, raise separate flags for team or staff improvement activity. Use special control points of supervisor.

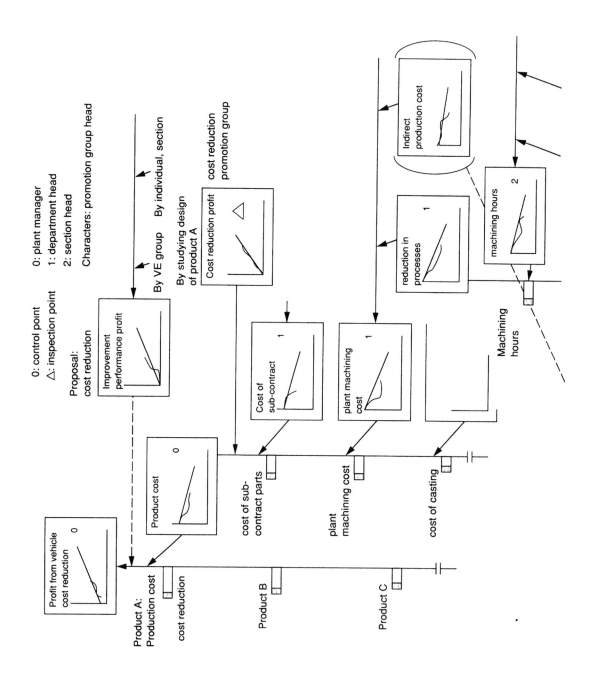

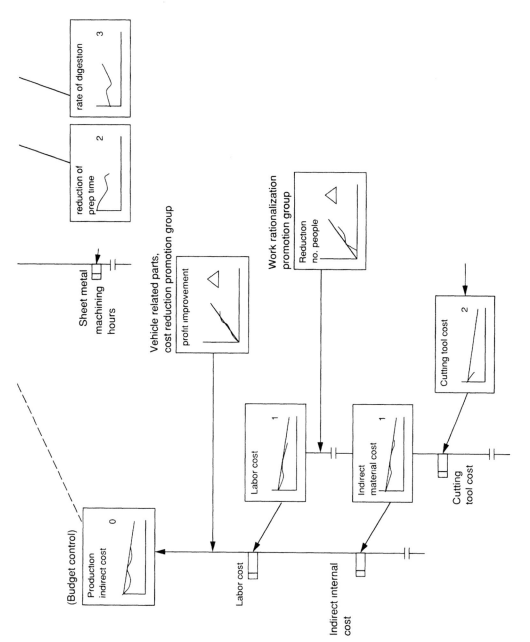

Figure 2-8. Target Deployment by Flag Method for Cost Reduction (Komatsu)

A *handling limit line* (not based on statistical methods) of the control graph in Figure 2-9 corresponds with the *control limit line* in a control chart.

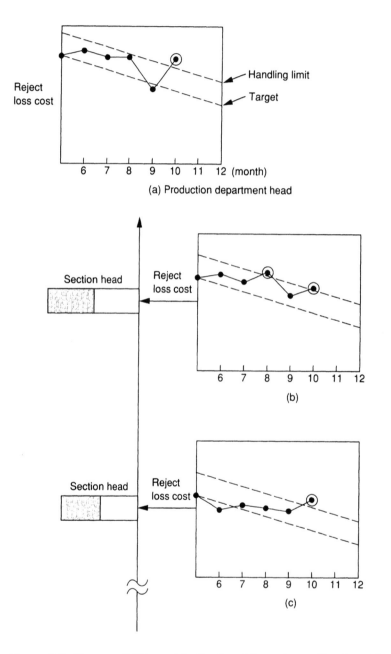

Figure 2-9. Responsibility and Authority of Department Head and Section Heads

Various QC methods — the Pareto chart, the fishbone diagram, and the control graph — have been combined in these figures to good effect.

The means to achieve the target should be planned as measures for the factors gleaned from QC problem solving. At the same time, there may be several measures for one factor, so selecting the best one is important.

Using the Top-to-bottom Method to Make a Policy Plan

The policy plan needs to be made in a top-to-bottom manner. That is, those jobs at the top must exhibit more leadership. To this end, repeated coordination of top-to-bottom policy plan drafts (especially strategic level target setting), bottom-to-top drafts (especially setting of conservative lower target values), and eventually final decisions by the president or a senior executive are necessary. For example, the president's preliminary policy might be distributed for preparation of preliminary policy sheets for each job classification. Then coordination of the president's final policy and the policies for job classifications are prepared. This works like a two-stage rocket.

Meeting to Coordinate the Various Job Classes and Related Departments

Generally, the policy plans to be implemented among the upper and lower job classifications and related departments are coordinated. Usually, discussions between the related persons and related departments are an effective approach.

Making Quick and Flexible Policy Plan Revisions

A policy plan should not be rigid. It should be revised as needed, depending on changes in the economy, the market, or the company itself.

Analyzing the Previous Year's Results for Policy Planning

Too often a policy or action plan consists of either haphazardly selected means without targets or, more simplistically, of targets without means. Missing is the QC-like solution to critical problems and the collection and analysis of information — the collection and preparation of "ingredients" for a "recipe."

The relationships among a series of items (for example, your supervisor's policy from last year, your own policy, an analysis of last year's results, an analysis of factors, and weights of factors) for planning a policy (target and means) is given in Figure 2-10.

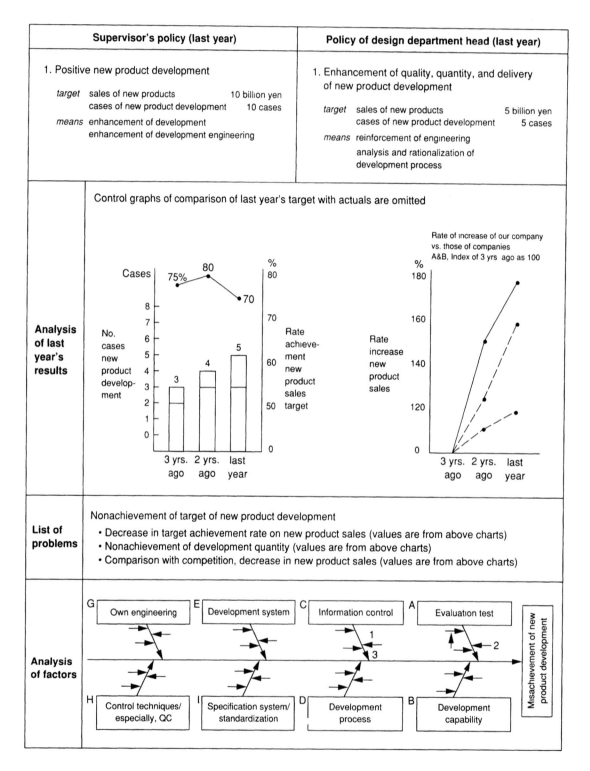

Supervisor's policy (last year)	Policy of design department head (last year)
1. Positive new product development *target* sales of new products 10 billion yen cases of new product development 10 cases *means* enhancement of development enhancement of development engineering	1. Enhancement of quality, quantity, and delivery of new product development *target* sales of new products 5 billion yen cases of new product development 5 cases *means* reinforcement of engineering analysis and rationalization of development process

Analysis of last year's results

Control graphs of comparison of last year's target with actuals are omitted

List of problems

Nonachievement of target of new product development
- Decrease in target achievement rate on new product sales (values are from above charts)
- Nonachievement of development quantity (values are from above charts)
- Comparison with competition, decrease in new product sales (values are from above charts)

Analysis of factors

Figure 2-10. Relationship among Requirements for Policy Planning

Critical factors .	Factor "A. Evaluation Test" (ex.)
	
	1. Misarrangement of test items (especially for below items)
	  • New quality problems after start of new product sales
	  • Major claims in the market
	  • Many new quality requirements from major users
	  • Change in market conditions or usage conditions for product
	
	2. Lack of study and system of evaluation test method
	  • Many quality problems difficult to test
	  • Many quality problems for which test method is not appropriate
	
	3. Lack of test equipment
	  • As a result of 20 new product developments of the past, contribution of evaluation test is more than engineering capability or information control and relation of good process (sufficient test)
	  → good result (good sales of new product) and poor process (insufficient test) → poor result (poor sales) was proven.

Arrangement of factors (weighing by Pareto analysis)	A. Vagueness or insufficient evaluation test
	  1. Poor arrangement of test items
	  2. Poor study and system of test method
	  3. Poor test equipment
	B. Insufficient equipment capability
	  (B-1 analysis result — omitted)
	C. Lack of collection
	D. Poor analysis, standardization of development process (procedure)
	E. Delayed arrangement of development system
	F. Delayed arrangement of specification system
	G. Poor use of own engineering
	H. Too little emphasis on control engineering
	I. Others
	
	Note: Degrees of contribution of factors A-I are converted to points
	
	Expected result through above improvement items rate of achievement target· 95% (100% max.)

	Priority measures	**Target**	**Present**

Design policy, department head (this year)	1. Planned and efficient achievement of new product development target
	*basic target** New product sales - New product cases
	priority policy
	
	1 Arrangement-enhancement of evaluation test
	  1. Arrangement of test item (4 items)
	  2. Systemization-development of test method (3 items)
	  3. Introduction-use of new test equipment (separate plan)
	2. Improvement of development engineering capability
		7 billion
		6 cases
			5 billion
			4 cases

* As a result of coordination between upper and lower classes, and to compete with competitors, challenge to 150% increase in target achievement to last year's performance was decided upon.

Points of Caution in Step 4

1. As policy deployment has gained popularity, many companies have published their own terminology and methods. Merely copying the practices of other companies will often lead to failure. Each company has its own reasons for the way it does things. That is why it is important that a company base its terminology and methods on QC-like controls and improvements.
2. The strong point of policy deployment is its application of QC-like methods to critical problems. Thus, it is indispensable to collect and analyze data according to QC principles.
3. Do not make the mistake of just filling in a premade form or chart and calling it a policy paper, action plan sheet, or control item list.

Step 5: Set Control Items and Prepare a Control Item List

1. Set control items for policy deployment when making a policy plan.
2. Draw up a control item list that specifies jobs, person in charge, frequency of control (interval, cycle, time period), control method, control data, emergency handling criteria, and other pertinent categories.
3. Throughout this process, coordinate with your immediate supervisor, subordinates, and other related department personnel.

Step 6: Deploy the Policy

Once you have made the policy plan (target and means), deploy it to the departments and job positions.

Seven-year Control Items for Policy Deployment

Control items for policy deployment are often set on the basis of policy plan achievements and can be divided into two categories:

1. Control points for checking by results
2. Inspection points or checkpoints for checking the factors (means) for target achievement

Preparation of the Control Item List

In recent practice, companies prepare the control item list along with the policy sheet and action plan sheet (or implementation plan sheet) rather than preparing it separately. In any case, further detail on the control items, including items for daily control, will be given in the next chapter.

Deployment of the Basic Policy Plan

Deployment of the policy plan (target and means) requires thorough coordination of all job classifications within each department and among related departments. The lower the job classification, the more detailed and specific the plan will be. Use of fishbone diagrams and system charts at this stage can be helpful in clarifying the relationship between targets and means.

The Target-Means Matrix: Its Purpose and Some Examples

As was mentioned in Chapter 1, it is important to check the means to see whether they really serve the intended purposes and targets. This entails some checking of inhibiting factors in the factor system process — checking that is based on an analysis of variance in last year's results.

Another point to remember is that often the target (purpose) and means (steps) are not clarified. Generally, using a matrix (two-dimensional chart) is effective for studying the relationship between heterogeneous subjects; the *target-means matrix* brings together the targets and means in matrix form.

To better understand the target-means matrix and its use in clarifying the cause-and-effect relationship between deployment of means and targets, refer to the Kobayashi Kosei case study in Chapter 5. At this point, however, consider the example of another company. Hokuriku Kogyo, which won the Deming Prize for small industries in 1984, manufactures forgings for construction machinery and automotive parts. Its TQC committee is active in deploying policy and in preparing and deploying priority action item charts, department action plans (Figure 2-11), and lists of control items (Figure 2-12). They use a target-means matrix that is uniquely adapted to their company.

Daily Control and **Hoshin Kanri**

Daily control. The concept of daily control evolved during the early 1960s, when TQC was in its formative stages. Companies began emphasizing the integration of QC in daily work; at the time, expressions such as "close to daily work" were actually more common than "daily control."

Before long, however, the concept of QC in daily work evolved into the concept of control by department, and thus policy deployment was born.

Control by department and by cross-functional management. Control by department by itself was found not strong enough to achieve company targets, so in the

Date ( )	Action Plan Sheet		Code
Material Section			△ X △ X △ X △ X

Upper-level Policy	Priority Action Item	Control Item	
		Characteristics	**Unit**
1. Building in of quality by factor-control for critical process	1.1 Reduce poor shearing • Reduce poor shearing of shear 100 A (improve stopper) • Reduce saw-cut rejection • Improve process capability	Rate of rejection of shears Rate of rejection of cut	% pcs.
	a. No. of cases of maintenance of process capability per machine	Rate of rejection of cut Process capability	pcs. cases
	1.2 -0- reject material	Maintenance rate	
	a. testing by spark test	No. of cases material rejection	cases
2. Productivity study by accumulation of cost improvement ideas	2.1 Improve cutting yield by ordering double-size steel material • list-up of feasible double size from production requests	No. of order issuance	points

Review date	Notes	Performance					Plan			
		Check date					Date			
		Plant manager	Section head	Group head	Chief	Person in charge	Plant manager	Group head	Chief	Group head

(plan) actual					Person in charge of promotion	Dead-line	Schedule									
prev. year, actual	Jan-Jun 1984	Jan-Jun 1984	Jul-Dec 1984	Jul-Dec 1984			$^{59}/_6$	7	8	9	10	11	12	$^{60}/_1$	2	3	4
0.013	(0.010)		(0.008)		Section head											
16	(8)				Group head											
14			(7)		Group head											
	(10)		(10)		Group head											
0	(0)		(0)		Section head											
6	(3)		(3)		Section head											
6	(6)		(6)		Section head											

(improvement) ------→ (implementation)

360-ton shear (100A) ------→

Test

Figure 2-11. Department Action Plan (Hokuriku Kogyo)

No.	Work	Class-ification	Control Item Characteristics	Unit	Person in charge	Control interval
1	Ordering	C	Rate of reduction of outsource cost	%	Section head	6 mo.
		C	Amount of outsource cost	million	Chief	mo.
2	Material (steel) ordering	C	No. of orders for double-size material	yen	Section head	mo.
3	Receiving	Q	Receiving rejection rate	point	Section head	mo.
		Q	Quantity of rejects received	%	Chief	mo.
		Q	Rate of attachment of inspection tag	pcs	Chief	mo.
		D	Rate of keeping to schedule of delivery	%	Section head	mo.
		D	Delay	%		

Date ( ) Material Section Control Items List

	Date prepared	
	Plant manager	Section head

Report to	Reporting interval	Reporter	Disposition criteria	
Cost control committee	6 mo.	Section head	$2.0 \begin{smallmatrix}+1.0\\-0.5\end{smallmatrix}$ (60/5)	Plant manager
Inspection	mo.	Chief		
Cost control committee	mo.	Section head	1 point/month $\begin{smallmatrix}+2.0\\-0\end{smallmatrix}$ (60/5)	
QA committee	mo.	Section head	$0.12\% \begin{smallmatrix}+2.02\\-0.04\end{smallmatrix}$ (60/5)	
Inspection	mo.	Chief		
Inspection	mo.	Chief	$100\% \begin{smallmatrix}+0\\-2.0\end{smallmatrix}$ (60/5)	
Production control committee	mo.	Section head	0.8	
Inspection				

Reporting

Figure 2-12. List of Control Items (Hokuriku Kogyo)

early 1960s the concepts of cross-functional management and control systems were born. For example, Musashi Kogyo University Director K. Ishikawa (1986) compared the organization to woven cloth. He argued, in the same way that cloth is made stronger through the weaving together of warp and woof, or horizontal and vertical, so will the organization be strengthened through the warp and woof of control by department and cross-functional management.

Toyota Motors put this theory into practice with the introduction of a two-dimensional chart for control by department and cross-functional management (Figure 2-13). Among the most well-known control systems are that of Komatsu — which uses QA to link quality (Q), cost (C), delivery (D), profit control (cost control), and production control — and that of Toyota Motors, which uses QA based on the concept of good quality at an appropriate price with cost controls.

The following points are important to the promotion of cross-functional management.

- QA will function at the core and be the most important function. A function committee or function meeting is established as an adjunct to the TQC committee or management meeting. Members are usually senior managers at the vice-president level or above.
- Cross-functional management evolved as a way to integrate company issues of quality, profit, and cost targets and to clarify the roles and responsibilities of each department.
- Once the critical problems for each function are known and a functional policy (target and means) determined as the means to solve the problem, then that functional policy must be built into the departmental policy in order to be implemented. The setup and use of control items are done accordingly.
- The results of cross-functional management are analyzed once or twice a year by committee members selected at a functional meeting or by a function committee, or the analysis can be done as a part of the president's or top management's audit.

Policy deployment and cross-functional management. Cross-functional management was not fully workable until it was coupled with the revolutionary concept of *hoshin kanri*, originated at Bridgestone Tire company. Bridgestone's company-wide system was based on the Japanese concepts of control by department and cross-functional management.

A 1962 survey of Deming Award recipient companies for TQC introduction clarified the model for policy deployment. At the same time, the system was regarded as a strong control system (step) for revolutionary management techniques

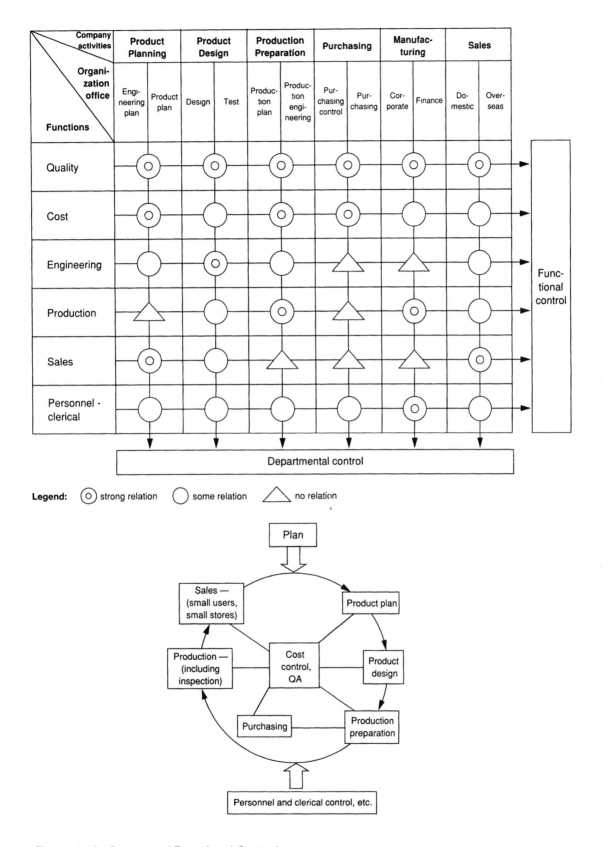

Company activities / Organization office / Functions	Product Planning		Product Design		Production Preparation		Purchasing		Manufacturing		Sales	
	Engineering plan	Product plan	Design	Test	Production plan	Production engineering	Purchasing control	Purchasing	Corporate	Finance	Domestic	Overseas
Quality	◎		◎		◎		◎		◎		◎	
Cost	◎		○		◎		◎		○		○	
Engineering	○		◎		○		△		△		○	
Production	△		○		◎		△		◎		○	
Sales	◎		○		△		△		△		◎	
Personnel - clerical	○		○		○		○		◎		○	

Functional control

Departmental control

Legend: ◎ strong relation   ○ some relation   △ no relation

Plan

Product plan

Product design

Production preparation

Purchasing

Cost control, QA

Production — (including inspection)

Sales — (small users, small stores)

Personnel and clerical control, etc.

Figure 2-13. Concept of Functional Control

that would promote a free trade policy and the strength necessary for international competition.

In September 1964, policy deployment was recognized as an official system with the establishment of the first TQC plan (including medium-term plans). In February and March of 1965, *hoshin kanri* was made an official term. *The Hoshin Kanri Manual* (company regulations) was published by Bridgestone in July.

Cross-functional management has been under study and in trial since the end of 1965, and in 1966 cross-functional management based on QCD (quality, cost, delivery) was implemented in the corporate offices and plants. It was some time, however, before the system was on track. Cross-functional management is more difficult to implement than control by department. At least this is true in Japan. Japanese society tends to be organized vertically, so control by department and hoshin planning come easily to us. We are weaker in horizontal organization, particularly in comparison with Americans or Europeans.

Ishikawa (1986) has said that a functional committee cannot be administered well without some revolution in the concepts for cross-functional management. This is true not only of the committee, however, but also of cross-functional management itself.

Use of daily control with hoshin kanri. Naming this new approach created controversy. At Bridgestone Tire, some people questioned the value of giving special recognition to the new system. In addition, the tendency of new control systems to separate workers from their daily jobs was feared with this as well.

At that time, the contents and scope of policy deployment were not clearly understood. For example, its relationship with other control systems (daily control, control by department, and cross-functional management) had not been clearly defined.

It was not until the period of low growth in the 1970s, when it became necessary to systematize and promote policy deployment, that the value of policy deployment became fully recognized. The uncertainties and the strong yen recession of the 1980s further advanced this movement. The result is that too much weight has been placed on policy deployment and daily control has begun to be forgotten. Table 2-7 and the relation chart in Table 2-8 give good definitions of daily, departmental, policy, and functional controls.

People unfamiliar with policy deployment often ask about its relationship to daily control. The best way to answer this might be to use the following analogy.

Daily control is like paying attention to one's health every day. Daily health controls include rising early, retiring to bed early, eating until you are only 80 per-

Table 2-7. Definitions of Daily Management (Departmental or Functional Management), *Hoshin Kanri*, **and Cross-functional Management**

Daily Management (Departmental or Functional Management)

Daily management can be defined as all the activities that each department must perform for itself on a daily basis that are necessary to most efficiently achieve their business goals. These activities are the most fundamental of business management.

NOTE: Daily management is no different than departmental or functional management Departmental or functional management may be easier to comprehend, but from the point of view of promoting TQC, daily management is the more familiar term to use.

Hoshin Kanri

Hoshin kanri can be defined as all organizational activities for systematically accomplishing the long- and mid-term goals as well as yearly business targets, which are established as the means to achieve business goals. In many cases, it is used for yearly targets.

Cross-functional Management

Cross-functional management can be defined as control activities that include planning for individual business elements like quality, cost, and delivery from a companywide (or business group) point of view. These are then implemented along with the daily management and hoshin activities of each department and the results are then evaluated throughout the company so that further action can be taken when necessary.

Table 2-8. Relationships among Various Controls

Classification	*Hoshin Kanri*	Daily Control	Relationship	
Departmental control	◎	◎	Imple-mentation	Imple-mentation
Cross-functional management	◎	◎	Plan/assess	Plan/adjust
Per product control	◎	○		

◎ strong relation   ○ some relation

cent full, drinking in moderation, and exercising. Policy deployment, on the other hand, is like paying attention to critical events such as illnesses or surgery. It also includes long-term health measures such as buying a membership in a sports club. Policy deployment identifies these critical items from among the daily control items and improves them. The same control items are set up for both daily control and policy deployment.

Points of Caution in Step 6

1. Policy deployment relies on the application of QC-like solutions to critical problems.
   - The success of policy deployment depends on the deployment of critical items.
   - A target is the expected result of the solution of a critical problem.
   - The means are the "measures of the factors" that are derived from analysis — that is, the measures for solving critical problems.
2. Problems that exist across departmental lines or problems with cross-functional management can be stratified in a list, as shown in Table 2-9. Note that corrective measures are indicated as well as the problems.

Table 2-9. List of Problems

Class-ifica-tion	Problems			Corrective Measures							Instruction of . . . head			
							Department in charge							
	Char-acter-istics	Causes	ABC	Content	Target	ABC	Own	Others	Name of team/circle	Dead-line	Yes/no	Content	Target	ABC
%	Year	List of problems	Business department / department . . . plant	. . . team / QC circle	In-charge member						Depart-ment head	Section head	Pre-pared by

Note: Classification is for major items so policy or major characters are filled in, e.g., quality, cost, delivery, productivity, etc.

Source: K. Ishihara (1984).

3. Although measures of the factors are important, terms such as "a lack of education" or "enhancing education" are too abstract to be used in policy deployment. Left unspecified, for example, is *who* is to be educated (directors, department or section heads, managers, staff) and *what type* of education (knowledge, product, engineering, production, methods, work) needs to be provided.
4. For proper formation of a policy plan, appropriate target and means must be set. Use of the target-means matrix can help you achieve this end.
5. Successful policy deployment depends on proper administration of the system.

Following are some examples of poor administration. This often happens in companies that receive no guidance in QC from specialists and attend no QC seminars. These examples, drawn from sales or clerical areas, are not published often. The reasons for lack of success in policy deployment are always the poor collection and analysis of information, an essential precondition to planning policy.

Example 1: Deployment without a Good Foundation

This example's poor results were due to the poor collection and analysis of information (grasping critical problems and factors on the basis of self-inspection of the previous year's results and setting up measures for these factors). This is what is meant by "without a good foundation."

As shown in Table 2-10, a branch manager and section head use the same means and yet they lack targets. Since only one schedule is used throughout the year, their plan is too loose.

Also lacking is a thorough QC stratification and analysis of the distribution channel (by region, products, dealership, retail store) and specific target means, and a list of persons responsible for each job category.

Table 2-10. Deployment of Action Plan without Good Foundation

Supervisor's Policy (Tokyo Branch Manager)			Action Plan of Tokyo Branch Sales Section Head				
No.	Priority	Priority target	No.	Priority action item	Target	Person in charge	Annual schedule 1 2 3 4 5 6 7 8 9 10 11 12
1	Arrangement of distribution channel	(not filled in)	1	Expansion of sales network	(not filled in)	Head of group A	◄———► (Loose schedule)

Priority action item = means

Example 2: Tunnel (or Smoke-stack) Type of Deployment

Type A and type B of tunnel deployment (Tables 2-11 and 2-12) deploy only the target (strictly speaking, the target items, target values, and expected results) and not the means (for the causes of critical problems).

Table 2-12 (type B) shows the means at one glance, but the analysis is insufficient so the means are useful mostly for handling emergencies. What is needed are the basic factors and basic means for them (means for the factor system priority). Both A and B are poor substitutes for policy and plan (target and means). Moreover, the target term "market share up" is too abstract. Which region, which product, and which customer need to be specified.

Table 2-11. Tunnel Type with Target Deployment Only (Type A)

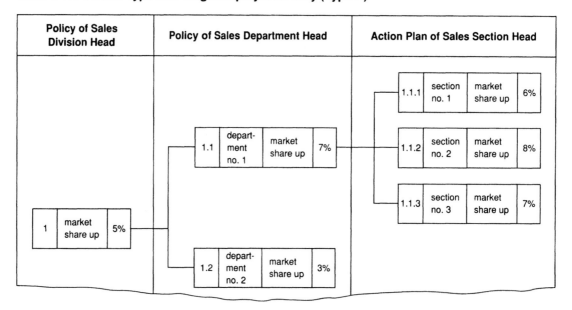

Example 3: Consolidated Tunnel Type of Deployment

Table 2-13 shows a type C, or consolidated tunnel, deployment policy. Here the target items and values (expected results) are shown at the same time. This is the tunnel, or smoke-stack, type. The schedule is loose, however.

Type D (Table 2-14) is better than type C, but only the target items are stratified (reports are stratified into "in-house," "between corporation and branches," and "between branch and dealerships"). Not set are factor analysis and the means by which reductions will be made. In short, stratification of the target is the only thing that has been done.

Table 2-12. Tunnel Type with No Pursuit of Causes (Type B)

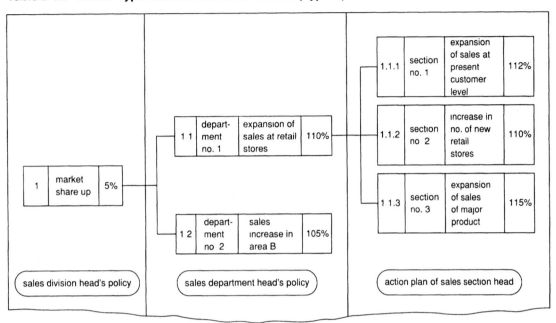

Table 2-13. Consolidated Tunnel Type (Type C)

	Supervisor's Policy Corporation Sales Plan Department			Corporate Sales Plan Section, Action Plan				
No.	*Hoshin* priority	Priority target	No.	Priority action item (means)	Current value	Target	Annual schedule	
							1 2 3 4 5 6 7 8 9 10 11 12	
1	Simplification of reports	30% reduction	1	Simplification of reports	— — —	30% reduction	Carry on to next year ◄——►	

Example 4: Policy Deployment at a Branch Office

Tables 2-15 and 2-16 are examples of policy deployment at the Osaka branch office of company X. They go one step beyond the policy deployment shown in previous examples (Tables 2-10 through 2-14).

First, the critical problems are listed and evaluated based on an analysis of the previous year's results by the branch head and the section head. Then as shown in Table 2-15, critical tasks are deployed (the bones). Table 2-16 is a further stratification (the muscle), an arrangement and analysis of Table 2-15. However, the person in charge and the schedule are omitted.

Table 2-14. Consolidated Type with Layers of Target Items Only and without Means (Type D)

No.	Supervisor's Policy (Department Head's Sales Plan) Priority	Target	No.	Action Plan of Tokyo Branch Sales Section Head Priority action item (means)	Target	Person in charge	Annual schedule 1 2 3 4 5 6 7 8 9 10 11 12
1	Simplification of reports	30% reduction	1	Expansion of sales network 1. reduction in in-house reports 2. reduction in reports between corporation and branches 3. reduction of reports between branch and dealerships	Annual increase of 10% " "	30% reduction 40% reduction 30% reduction 20% reduction	Study of Action on status reduction ◄──►◄──► Study of Action on status reduction ◄──►◄──► (plan to act on in next year)

Table 2-15. *Hoshin Kanri* at Osaka Branch of Company X (Skeleton)

Osaka Branch Head's Policy

(Expansion of sales)
 	
1. Enhancement of sales power
  • Promotion of prioritized sales means
  • Sales of suitable products to customers
 	
2. Enhancement of QA system

Sales Section Head's Action Plan

1.1 Enhancement of sales power
  • Promotion of increase of low market share
  • Promotion of prioritized sales
  • Arrangement of sales network
  • Improvement of user approach
 	
2.2 Promotion of QA action
  • Collection of quality information
  • Reduction in branch office claims

Table 2-16. *Hoshin Kanri* at Osaka Branch of Company X (Flesh)

Osaka branch, sales section head's action plan

Supervisor's Policy (Osaka Branch Head)	Target			Priority Action Items
	Target item	Target value	Current values	
1. Sales expansion, target, product A, 12 billion yen, product B, 10 billion yen, product C, 8 billion yen (priority means) 1.1 Enhanced sales power 1. priority sales 2. suitable product teasers 1 2 Enhancement of QA system (rest omitted)	1. Sales, expansion weight ( ) 30% target value	Product A, 12 billion yen • increase of market share 20% • new product sales to large users 120% up to last year and 5 new retail stores • user satisfaction (total) > 90 points	last year actual 10 billion yen share 10% last year actual ( ) 100% < 70 points	1.1 Proven sales enhancement *1.1.1 Prioritized sales* 1) Increase of low market share • Study of dispersion in shares • Study of low market share district/users (attack targets) • Study of strong competitor's sales method Improvement of weakness 2) Large users • Study of large users at which competition is stronger • Preparation of "large user map" (related to [1]) • New product sales to weak large users 3) Arrangement of retail network • New retail stores (for weak district) • Education of store managers, employees (example) Planned sales (medium-term plan, annual plan, plans control), sales engineering, labor control (morale improvement), finance • Reduction of dispersion among retail stores 1.1.2 Study and improvement of user approach method (customer) 1) Study user satisfaction (total) • Arrange user cards (related to 1) • Specific user needs by 2.1 (3) 2) Planned visits of users, improved approach, "key man" 3) Prepare failure examples, clarify failure factors, prevent repeats (intentional prevention)
2. Enhancement of QA system (target and means, omitted)	2. Promotion of QA activity wt. < > 25%, value	• cases of info collection > 30/mo. • number of product plan proposals, > 3/mo. • > 90, user satisfaction • < 4/mo. claims of branch office account		2.1 Increased collection and quality of information 1) Study of method of collection 2) Information related to new product 3) Collection, analysis of user needs (prepare list) 2.2 Quality emphasis (market in) on sales service 1) User satisfaction 2) Team work between salesmen and servicemen, systematizing 3) Branch office claims (inventory, poor quality due to transportation, lack of user service)

Step 7: Deploy the Control Items

The deployment of control items, particularly of *hoshin kanri* items, is related to the making of policy and plan. Furthermore, it is an outgrowth of step 5, in which control items are established. (The particulars of setting control items are covered in the next chapter.) But what happens when control items are set up and deployed by people who have not attended QC seminars? A typical result is a deployment of mandatory control items (Tables 2-17 and 2-18).

Table 2-17. Control Items of Sales Department Head and Sales Section Head (Poor Example)

Target		Priority Action Item	Control Items (for target)	
Item	Target value			
1. Product knowledge (especially engineering)	3 seminars in one year	1.1 Holding of seminar for product knowledge (especially engineering)	3 seminars in one year	
		1.2 Prepare product manual		

Table 2-18. Outsourcing Section Head's Action Plan

Policy of Material Department Head	Section Head's Target	Section Head's Prioritization Item	Control Item	Control Value	Control Method	
					Frequency	Control data
1. Reduction of quality accident from outsource *target* 50% of last year	Reduction in claims *target* 50% of last year	1 Prevention of claims of worst 2 companies	Worst 2 companies, corrective measure meeting	50% of last year	Monthly	(not filled in)
		2. Claim reduction meeting	action plan	one/week	Weekly	(not filled in)
		3 Elimination of own company's claims				

Poor Deployment of Control Items: Analysis

Table 2-17 was based on a policy from the president but was prepared by the sales department and section heads as a part of their own job responsibilities, and so the control items are identical.

The problem was based on differences in product knowledge of the skilled and the nonskilled sales staff. Although the sales department held seminars and planned a manual, it failed to perform QC analysis of the knowledge disparity, and so its control items were identical to those of the sections heads. Had the sales department heads performed QC information collection and analysis (Step 3) they would have discovered that salespeople with poor knowledge cannot respond well to the users' questions. This fact could be a live control item, for example, "5 nonanswers per month." A Pareto analysis often shows the problem to be above 50 percent in the top 5 to 10 items. This can be the base for further education or preparation of manuals. Another control item might be the scores on tests given after seminars, for example, "80 percent of class attendees have A's."

Points of Caution in Step 7

1. When there is a lack of knowledge and experience, then the mandatory creation or bringing about of an action plan as part of one's job responsibility will produce policy deployment control items like those shown in Table 2-18.
2. Under such circumstances, very often mistaken control items may be listed. Look at the *control items* row. Irrelevant control items occurred for the two worst companies in the *corrective measures meeting* and the *action plan sheet.* There are often cases where control items in the control sheets of the control methods (such as the *kaizen* improvement action plan) are improperly accounted for or just wrong.
3. Which item do we check in the action plan sheet? At the corrective measures meeting, which items become priorities to be checked? Or with the QC approach, *grasping the current situation* and *cause analysis* may be emphasized. If PDCA is truly practiced, though, well-founded control items should naturally float to the surface.
4. For beginners of control item deployment, try not to make control items too technical or serious. The important thing is to set control items on points of control, where there is a knack for control, or items that keep you awake at night if the results of checking do not turn out well.
5. Table 2-19 is an advanced example of setting the control items from Table 2-18.

Step 8: Implement the Policy Plan

Implement based on the policy plan or *hoshin* sheet or the action plan sheet. Implementation varies from company to company. No implementation format can be prescribed over any other; rather it must arise from the culture and the purpose of the company itself.

Table 2-19. Outsourcing Section Head's Action Plan (Control Item of *Hoshin Kanri*)

Material Department Head's Policy *Target*	Section Head's Action Plan	Control Item:	Control Level		Control Method	
			Target (handling limit)	Check frequency	Action	Data
1. Reduction in quality problems of received products, critical quality problems < > No. -0- cases (rest omitted)	1. Reduction of critical claims, no. -0- cases	Critical claims	-0- case (1 case)	Monthly	In case of beyond control level 1. Study of factor (outsource section - QA section) 2. Plan for repeat prevention - (committee) action (contractor) check (committee) check (committee) check (committee)	No. of critical claims, control graph
	1) Prevention of repeats • QA diagnosis of problem contractor • QC seminar for all contractors (once/1/4 yr.) In-house: - meeting for prevention of repeat (committee)	"	"	"		"
	2) Promotion of prevention of repeats, worst 2 companies • survey (monthly) • guidance (case by case)	Parts adhesion quality defects	-0- case (1 case)	Each time of defect (regular) 2 times /mo.	" "	Defective parts, adhesion, Control graph,
	2. Elimination of in-house quality defects, no. cases, -0- cases	Omitted	Omitted	Omitted	Omitted	Omitted

Step 9: Check the Results of Implementation

1. Compare the target with the actual results and check the difference. A difference or disparity between the target value and the actual value is called a problem.
2. When there are differences, analyze the process (work method) and find the cause.
3. Act on those causes that have the greatest effect (take a corrective measure).
4. If the corrective measure succeeds, incorporate it into next year's plan so that it can be maintained. If it fails, note it in next year's plan so it will not be repeated.
5. Prepare the policy (plan) status report or the CA (check-action) report when necessary in order to report on the results of implementation.

Understanding the Problems

A problem is a disparity between the expected results and the actual results. In this sense, a large disparity means a critical problem.

Check the problem. If the problem is critical, you need to check the policy plan. A check should be performed on a regular basis — that is, quarterly, monthly, weekly, or daily — and coordinated among various job classifications. Then you need to study the results of those checks. Recently, this has often been done at meetings attended by business departments, divisions, and business offices (for example, plants, branch offices, and sales offices). The results of the QC diagnosis (made by the president, top manager, or department head), are incorporated into these studies.

Take action. When you find disparity between the target and the actual situation, analyze the process (work method) for factors that are to be acted on (corrected). For example, if a check should reveal bad results (nonachievement of the target), act to recover the nonachieved portion or to prevent repetition. If a check should reveal good results (achievement of the target or better), act to maintain those results (through quarterly, semi-annual, or annual checks).

These are the primary actions for *hoshin kanri*. To continue the hoshin cycle you must return to STEP 3 at this point (see Figure 2-14). Next, a QC diagnosis and the level of hoshin planning is explained in relationship to checking on the disposition of the policy deployment results, and the final step — the status report — is defined.

Making a QC Diagnosis

The audit versus the diagnosis. QC audits were popular in the 1960s, until they were superseded in the 1970s by QC diagnoses. In the 1980s, the word *diagnosis* became quite general. Bridgestone used top diagnosis when the company decided to implement *hoshin kanri*. That first diagnosis occurred in February of 1965. It was selected on the basis of the theory shown in Table 2-20.

The purpose and guidelines for diagnosis by the top (hoshin kanri). Top diagnosis (diagnosis by top management) helps top management to understand the good points and the problems (management control, product quality, work quality) of policy deployment through questions concerning promotion and understanding of TQC by top management. Policy deployment diagnosis proceeds according to the following guidelines.

1. Determine the degree to which targets are achieved — that is, the extent to which top policy on matters such as management, quality, and QC policies has been deployed.
2. In your evaluation, look not only at results but at the process for achieving results. Do not limit praise to good results, and do not scold if results are bad.
   - A good process means a praiseworthy work method.
   - Bad results need clarification of the causes and the bad process.

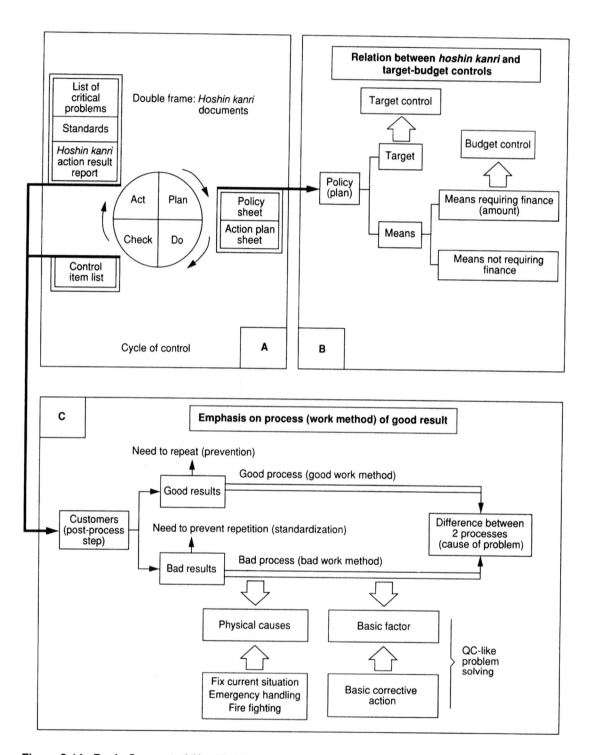

Figure 2-14. Basic Concept of *Hoshin Kanri*

Table 2-20. Audit and Diagnosis

Classification	Audit	Diagnosis
Person in charge of carrying out	Third parties • audit department and the auditor within the company, or QC personnel in an American company	Person who determined the policy • president, executives, directors, division and department heads, and office manager
Evaluation and judgment standards	Exist • example: various standards and checklists such as QA (or QC) standard manuals are specified in American companies	Nothing specific exists • although the manuals and checklists are written by each company, they are used in a flexible manner • they are often written with the "Deming Award Checklist" used as a reference
Evaluation and actual practice	• judgment of O or X, or "good" or "no good," is made by referring to the above standards • audit is completed by a third party evaluation (reporting the audit results to the instructing authority after evaluation), and the auditor would not get involved in actual practices (improvements)	• pointing out mostly the important issues through listening to the reports and stories of the persons being diagnosed • after the diagnosis is made, each diagnosing person is like a doctor and each person being diagnosed is like a patient. They develop a cure (problem-solving method) on their own
Notes	(1) The etymology of the word "audit" means to listen to, to investigate, and to evaluate (2) Dr. Asaka (professor with honors at Tokyo University) proposes and practices a QC examination based on the belief that an examination is necessary before the diagnosis.	

  • Praise of efforts made and encouragement are needed in order to prevent repetition of mistakes. See, for example Corner C in Figure 2-14.
3. Keep in touch with the departments being diagnosed.
  • Recognize and praise the departments being diagnosed for their capability in analysis, problem solution, and control.
  • If the target is not achieved, clarify the reasons for failure and study the problems in terms of planning the target means. At the same time, offer advice and instruction.
4. Listen to your subordinates. Judge and evaluate fairly.
5. Use the results of a diagnosis to study companywide critical problems, take corrective measures, and perform companywide PDCA.

The Effects of Top Diagnosis

Various benefits result from top diagnosis, including benefits related to human resources. Two are cited below.

- *Understanding those on the work floor:* Top management will actually go to the work floor for a question-and-answer period and to study. Such sessions differ from the usual meetings and reports. Each group makes presentations, but unlike more formal meetings, these are very lively sessions that test people's understanding.
- *Direct communication with the work floor:* Both a daytime session and an evening session (an intimate discussion between the diagnosing group and the receiving group) make for more meaningful communication.

For detailed discussions of QC diagnosis refer to the following sources: T. Asaka, et al. (1987); M. Kogure, et al. (1983); T. Nomi, et al. (1982); K. Fujita, et al. (1978).

There are two types of evaluation to consider:

- *Overall evaluation.* Overall evaluation of hoshin planning, which means evaluation of the policy plan, deployment, action taken, results, and so on, is carried out through policy deployment audit, or diagnosis, is also included. An example is that of Kobayashi Kosei, shown in Figure 2-15.
- *Level evaluation.* Table 2-21 gives an example of a level evaluation chart, which has become popular recently. Checklists are also used, but they are basically the same. Table 2-21 should, of course, be adapted to your own company.

Step 10: Prepare the Status Report for Implementing *Hoshin Kanri*

The status report is drawn up to report on the PDCA of this year's policy deployment. A report is made for each job, section, or department, as needed, and distributed to your supervisors or to related departments, including the policy deployment office.

Normally, the *hoshin* status report, or achievement report, is prepared after one PDCA of the policy deployment. It is usually a one-page report. Table 2-22 gives an example.

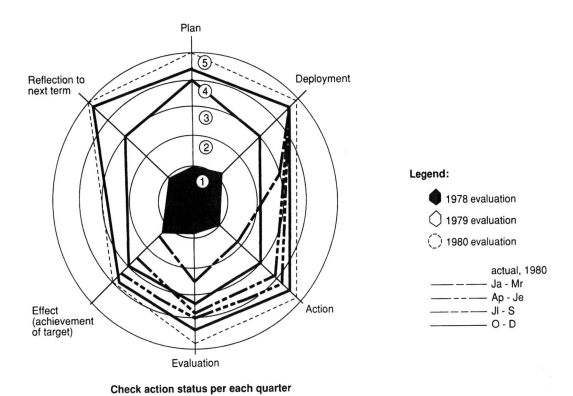

Check action status per each quarter

Evaluation criteria for *hoshin kanri*

Evaluation score	Criteria
5 pt.	Improvement is there, with good PDCA
4 pt.	Systematized work is stable with more than one PDCA cycle
3 pt.	System is completed, PDCA beginning to work
2 pt.	Each work method is arranged, overall interrelation is there
1 pt.	No planning in work, no overall relationship

Figure 2-15. Overall Evaluation of *Hoshin Kanri* (Kobayashi Kosei)

Table 2-21. Level Evaluation of *Hoshin Kanri*

• problem   - good point (or improved point)

Classification	Evaluation Levels (Stages)	
	1	2
Overall control system *quality policy, QC policy,* *hoshin kanri system, QA system*	• No overall control system (not clear) • No *hoshin kanri* • Unclear quality, QC (promotion policy - QA policy only plan of QC circle promotion) • Poor interdepartmental relationships	- Effort for overall control - *hoshin kanri* - quality assurance system - Partly clear quality policy, QC policy • Need for cross-functional management • No problem extraction • No match to improvement measures
Management strategy and long/medium-term plan *company motto basic concept* *management strategy* *long/medium-term plan*	• Company motto exists but not alive • Insufficient strategy • Long/medium-term plans (5-yr and 3-yr.) are not there • No long-term vision	- Company motto exists (basic concept is clarified) - Long/medium-term policy based on strategy is there Information is being collected • Plans of department are not streamlined No companywide policy is clear
Planning of policy-plan on self-inspection	• No self-inspection of last year (collection and analysis of information) • Theme is sporadic • Only results are evaluated • No process-oriented concept	- Self-inspection of last year is done - Some policy-plan is clear • Collection of data, type, and quantity are insufficient • Weak work on critical problems, weighing and study of factors
Analysis capability *Problem solution capability*	• Haphazard and no plan	• Abstract policy-plan, weak base of target-means • Budget control is separated from *hoshin kanri*
Setup of control items	• No items are set • No understanding of control items (definition)	- Each job sets control items • Control value of item is abstract • Same items for supervisor and subordinate, of tunnel type
Coordination and deployment *policy-plan* *control item*	• No coordination between superior and subordinate • Loosely set policy-plan and control items • No consistency and thoroughness	- Some coordination - Some relation between supervisor and subordinate • Poor relationship with self-inspection of last year (check and analysis of critical problems)
Check-action of policy-plan	• No check of policy-plan (progress) • Handling of emergency is sporadic • Revision and issue of standards are few	- Difference between target and actual is studied (no analysis) - Standards are being issued • Review of policy-plan is not done • QC diagnosis is not done (diagnosis, hereunder) • Revision of standard is inactive
Model actions by supervisor and participation *Annual hoshin kanri*	• Negative attitude to *hoshin kanri* (no understanding) • Same as above for clerical, sales, and engineering depts.	- Positive attitude among superiors of production department - Partial participation at clerical, sales, and engineering depts. • Policy-plan cannot be set unless data from bottom is submitted, in general

Evaluation Levels (Stages)		
3	**4**	**5**
- Overall control - *hoshin kanri* - QA systems are there with actions - Clear quality, QC policies, plan - Effort on cross-functional management • Problems out of above systems are there but not enough corrective measures	- System chart for each system is there with good correlation - System of function is there - Long/medium quality - QC policies and promotion plan are there - Problems are extracted and properly dealt with	- Challenging work for excellence In all department/functions is there - Top - director - department/ section heads with good leadership - System among functions and administration rules are there with PDCA
- Deployment of basic concept is done - Strategy is clear (long/medium-term plan) - Basic target-means are clarified • Analysis of environment, long/medium-term, is weak	- Strategy is based on company motto and concept - Strategy and long/medium-term plan are compatible • Long/medium-term policy and annual policy-plan are not well related	- Leadership is strong for plan of strategy and plans - Rules for planning are there with PDCA - Good match between plan and policy - Above is based on quality-supreme concept
- Critical problems and factors are studied based on self-inspection - Target and means are set for problem solution - Integration of *Hoshin Kanri* and budget control is planned	- QC story is there for self-inspection and analysis - Policy-plan (target-means) are planned in relation to critical problems - Supervisor's and subordinate's policy-plan are well related	- Rules and system for planning of policy-plan based on self-inspection is there (system) - Control with emphasis on *hoshin kanri* is there and well related to budget control
• Weak in QC analysis and solution of problems • Policy-plans are mostly formality only • Weak connection between superior's and subordinate's policy-plan	• Still budget-control oriented, weak relation with profit plan	- Proper, timely correction of policy-plan against charges - Long/medium-term plan is related to policy-plan
- Connection between items for jobs is studied - Target value of items is clear • Handling limit of item is not clear	- Target value-handling limit of items are clear - Connection with policy-plan (target-means) is good • Setting up of items of daily control is good	- Rules for items of *hoshin kanri* and daily control are there - Revision is properly handled
- Setup based on supervisor policy-plan and control items - Related to self-inspection of last year • No check of relation to related departments	- Policy-plan, control items are set up with good check with related departments - Supervisor's policy-plan, items are used for setup • Coordination and deployment not system-like	- Rules for coordination of policy-plan and control items are there (system) - Consistency in deployment of policy-plan and control items
- Analysis of target/actual if QC - Regular QC diagnosis - Revision of standards is active • Feedback of check results to next year policy-plan is insufficient	- Feedback to next year is good, re: policy-plan, QCD - Not enough standards revision - Diagnosis (*hoshin kanri* audit) is done • Upstream check-action is insufficient • Control items are used and emergency handling is done	- Check-action procedures are ruled re: policy-plan (system) - Check-action at upstream is done
- Leadership of top of prod. dept. is there for *hoshin kanri* - Engineering dept. is getting active • Relation with and deployment to related company, dealers, etc. are weak • *Hoshin kanri* at clerical-sales depts. is separated from daily control	- Production and engineering depts. are both active for *hoshin kanri* - Engineering top is exhibiting good leadership for *hoshin kanri* - Clerical and sales are getting to be positive • Process-oriented view is insufficient	- Roles of supervisors for *hoshin kanri* are ruled - Clerical and sales are active in *hoshin kanri* - *Hoshin kanri* is related to related companies (or group companies as well) - *Hoshin kanri* is working in practice

Table 2-22. Items for *Hoshin Kanri* Status Report

Per Function (overall)	Per Theme
1. President's policy 2. Superior's policy 3. Department head's policy 　a. Target 　b. Priority 　c. Implementation status 　d. Effect 　e. Problems 　f. Future basic policy	1. Theme (policy-plan) 2. Selection of theme, reason 3. Current status 4. Target 5. Analysis 6. Priority means and status 7. Effect (1) tangible 8. Effect (2) improvement of system 9. Problems and future basic policy

CHAPTER 3

Control Items for *Hoshin Kanri*

The Role of Control Items in *Hoshin Kanri* Systems

Control Items Are Necessary to Run the Control Cycle

A cycle of control steps (PDCA) is a natural part of business planning systems or management planning systems; it is the means by which the company can plan target and means, make business plans, check results, and incorporate the results into the next year's business plan. Policy deployment uses PDCA to identify critical items for breakthroughs or for improvement. The following steps are followed:

1. Set up and deploy the target and means. *(Plan)*
2. Implement the means and solve critical problems. *(Do)*
3. Evaluate the performance and check progress toward the targets. *(Check)*
4. Standardize the results into daily controls or transfer them to re-improvement plans. *(Act)*

You can determine control items while setting up the target and means, and at the same time you can set up the control items to check the implementation of those means that contribute to achievement of the target. Then you use both types of control items to check the progress of the process while solving critical problems during the implementation stage. Moreover, you use them to evaluate the performance at the end of the business term (that is, to measure the control item's contribution toward target achievement). After analyzing any deviation in performance, you can transfer the evaluation to a maintenance control (daily control) or incorporate the results into the next year's target. If the target is not achieved, you analyze the factors and the control item data. Then you plan corrective measures and incorporate the results into next year's target-means matrix.

Control Items Are Necessary to Establish a Link to the Target

A policy (target-means) must be well understood by all employees before it can be thoroughly integrated in the company. An understanding by each employee of the relationship between his or her work and company targets is also necessary. Furthermore, reasonable targets must be set up, their positions clarified within both their vertical (top-to-bottom) and horizontal (interdepartmental) organization. This means establishing a network of control items or visible control items as a way to link the entire system of targets and means being deployed.

Control Items Are Necessary as a Condition for Voluntary Control

The principle of control is based on the idea that people are inherently good and want to perform optimally; therefore control must be voluntary. Voluntary control must satisfy the following conditions without exception.

1. There must be a clear understanding of the target to be achieved.
2. There must be a clear understanding of what steps are needed to achieve the target.
3. There must be a clear understanding of what steps are needed to address nonachievement of the target.

The latter two points need criteria to determine abnormality and handle anomaly in the control chart to arrive at the target. Voluntary control items satisfy these conditions, as well.

Definition of a Control Item

• an item selected as a subject of control for maintenance of product quality
• an item selected as a subject of control for rational control action in company-wide QC (for example, per each job classification control)

Further, according to K. Ishikawa, a control item is a yardstick that measures or judges the setting of a target level, the contents of the work, the process and the results of each stage of breakthrough, and improvement in control during management activity.

System of Control Items

The system of control items is shown in Figure 3-1; note that the types of checks are "checking with cause" and "checking with results."

Figure 3-2 shows a system conceived by J. M. Juran (1969), in which this basic structure is related to both policy deployment and daily control. A company's work can be divided into two categories: daily control (or maintenance control) and hoshin planning for breakthroughs and improvements.

The control level of the former is given from the control area. Policy deployment comes from improvement tasks with set targets. Both are treated as control

Proposed by:	System	Remark
General	Control item checkpoint (check by cause) control point (check with results)	Attention is required because names for basic structure of control items are different at different companies. No mistake occurs as long as the concept of basic structure is understood. These are some of the examples.

K. Ishikawa
(1979)
	Control items 1. Cause – checkpoint
	
	                2. Result – control character,
	                          control point	

K. Ishikawa and K. Koura (1979)	Control point, check item — check by cause, control item — Check with result (control point, checkpoint)	

Y. Akao
(1984)
	Control items, check item — items checked by cause
	                           control character —
	                           characters checked with
	                           result	

Y. Nayatani	Control items, those of factor system, those of result system	
N. Kano (1981, 1983)	Work checked with results when staff department plans for specific function, have it implemented companywide and called major work, and department in charge is called in-charge department, and those control items are called major items.	

Figure 3-1. System of Control Items

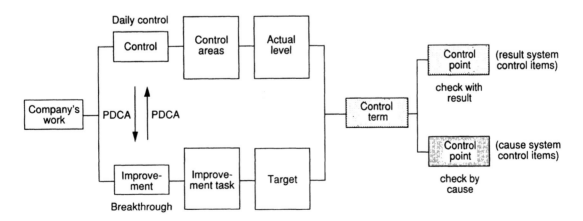

Figure 3-2. System of Control Items and *Hoshin Kanri* Daily Control (J.M. Juran 1969)

items, however. Control and improvement work together mutually during the PDCA cycle, like two wheels of a vehicle. Control items are further divided into control points that are checked against the results and checkpoints that are checked by the causes. The concept is based on management by process rather than objective; it is a case of checking the results of the work that is delegated from above. For the subordinate, the work result is a control point; for the supervisor, it is a factor system and a checkpoint. Also, the work of the management control office or the president's office that makes the business plan all have departmental plans that are based on the PDCA cycle. They have their results reported to them and checked by the offices in charge of the P(lan) and the C(heck), since the entire PDCA cycle is not done by them. In this case each checkpoint is called an *evaluation characteristic*. Performance of the entire PDCA cycle is the work of each individual; each control point of the results check of PDCA in this case is called a *control characteristic*. In these cases, the evaluation characteristics correspond to the major items listed by Kano in Figure 3-1.

Concept of Control Items

The checking of control items can be done according to causal systems and result systems. Control items are items whose work results must be checked at the check or control stage, as shown in Figure 3-3(a).

A check of the results and control characteristics appears in the fishbone diagram in Figure 3-3(b). The task at this stage is to look at the variance in the factor system (process), or the five M's (material, machine, method, man/woman, and measurement), and check the effects of the factors on the characteristics. You do this using the control chart and control graphs. Should you discover an anomaly, you analyze it and take action on that particular factor. This is called a control point. Normally, handling of a single factor is one of the items for work standards, but if it is done with a checklist or check chart, it is often called *advance control*, that is, action to prevent problem occurrence. In terms of the control cycle, this is similar to a small-scale PDCA in the planning and implementation stage, and it is checking for a cause. This is called a checkpoint.

A *control point* is used to analyze data and take action accordingly. A *checkpoint* requires immediate judgment and handling and must be checked on a daily basis.

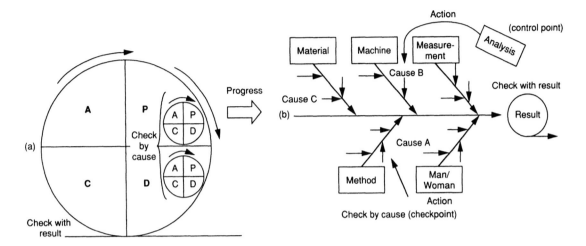

Figure 3-3. Concept of Control Item

According to Nayatani (1978), in policy deployment a control point can be called a control item with a target (result), whereas a checkpoint can be thought of as a control item with a means (factor).

Control items need a judgment criterion and a handling criterion for anomalies. You can use a control chart for the control points within the control items. Just as a control limit line is used in a control chart, so are judgment criteria and handling criteria for anomalies necessary for control points. Generally, you use the target value and plan line for daily control. Judgment criteria based on engineering findings must be set up for checkpoints.

As mentioned earlier, control items are used for both policy deployment and for daily control. Dr. Juran's concept limited control items to maintenance, as shown in Figure 3-2. But Komatsu and I expanded the concept to include improvement. Improvement and daily work are both integral to a company. Companywide improvements become a project, and when done on the shop floor, they can become a theme for a QC circle. Improvements on the current condition must be undertaken through policy deployment. There are also many daily work activities that support improvement activities, and these must be checked daily. Also, some of the control items will be common to both *hoshin kanri* and daily control, as Kano points out.

Advantages of Determining Control Items

The determination of control items for *hoshin kanri* and daily control requires close cooperation among all employees, and thus offers an opportunity for participation by everyone. Specifically, it offers the following advantages:

1. It prevents duplication of work by centralizing control.
2. It prevents neglect of any job by removing gaps in control.
3. Controls can be adjusted according to work priorities.
4. The interchange and meetings that occur during policy deployment improve communication among all levels.
5. Clarification and large-scale delegation of responsibility and authority promotes the development of human resources.
6. A better understanding of control is achieved, which leads to improved control capability. Often, the distinction between policy deployment and target control is questioned. Table 3-1 gives one answer based on the development process of control items, concepts of control, and target control in the behavioral sciences.
7. A control network is formed and the TQM system of participation by everyone and all departments is established (integrating all vectors and capabilities).
8. The areas in which QC techniques are used is expanded (control with data and facts, solution of problems using analysis).

Table 3-1. Evaluation of *Hoshin Kanri* and Target Control

Classification	Evaluation		Remarks
	Result	Process	
Hoshin kanri	◎	◎	Control based on concepts of respect for humanity and inherent goodness of people
Target control	◎	△	Motivation based on theory Y

The Origin of Control Items in *Hoshin Kanri*

Even when QC was introduced in Japan, its emphasis was on policy. Later, Teijin acted on the ideas of Juran and developed the list of control items. In 1964, at the Matsuyama QC conference, "control items based on policy plans" and "appropriate control items for improvement targets" were conceived. Control items for policy deployment, even though the term *hoshin kanri* had not yet been born, were germinating in the flag method developed by Komatsu and were further developed after Bridgestone Tire coined the term in the spring of 1965. I emphasized the role of control items in relation to target control, cross-functional management, and overall control systems. A number of efforts — including "control by allocation" in one case study and, at Kobe Steel and Matsushita Electronics, "QC policies, plans, development, and the role of staff" and "Operation Zelcoba" — also exist. Later came the development of deployments such as request items from department heads, used in the hoshin system at Ricoh. Kobayashi Kosei's target-means deployment matrix pursued the joining of target and means. Use of the seven QC tools integrated QC methodology into policy deployment. Later, Nayatani (1978) proposed the use of the seven *new* QC tools in policy deployment. These developments were extended with Comany's publication of *Hoshin Kanri Seven Tools* and their employee manual. Moreover, the relationship among policy deployment, daily control, and cross-functional management was clarified. This relationship is described in Chapter 4.

Target Deployment and Control Items

The flag method used at Komatsu can be called a Pareto deployment of targets using a fishbone diagram and Pareto charts. Figure 3-4 outlines the flag method. A large flag, such as reducing loss due to defects, is raised first for the plant manager. Next, a fishbone diagram (right) is prepared, showing the department heads, while a Pareto chart (left) is drawn up to show the size of the contributing factors. The cross-hatch portion indicates the targeted improvement. Thus, a flag for department A's head is made. A Pareto deployment for each product is also done, and project activities are performed in order to improve products A and B in accordance with the degree of contribution. This deployment continues in the QC circle, and action plans for each circle are prepared so that progress in the improvement activity can continue. Each large, medium, and small branch points in the direction of the central arrow, promoting cooperation and participation by everyone and clearly indicating their contribution to the plant manager's target. Operation Zelcoba at Matsushita Electronics, which began in 1975, developed a method for target-means deployment using a "control panel" that corresponds to the flag in the flag method. These steps are outlined in Figure 3-5.

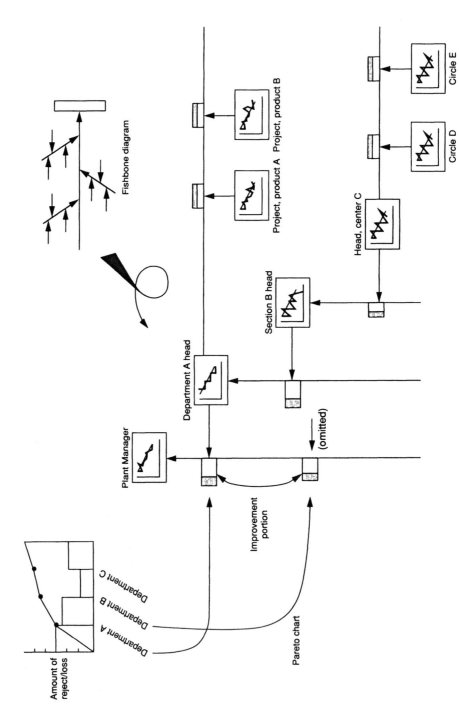

Figure 3-4. Pareto Deployment of Target in "Hata Method" at Komatsu

Outline of operation Zelcoba is shown with a model of production mode where one group is in charge of one product (from material to completion). In this case, the target for each product (each group) is set at <0.3% then target for section and plant become <0.3%, automatically.

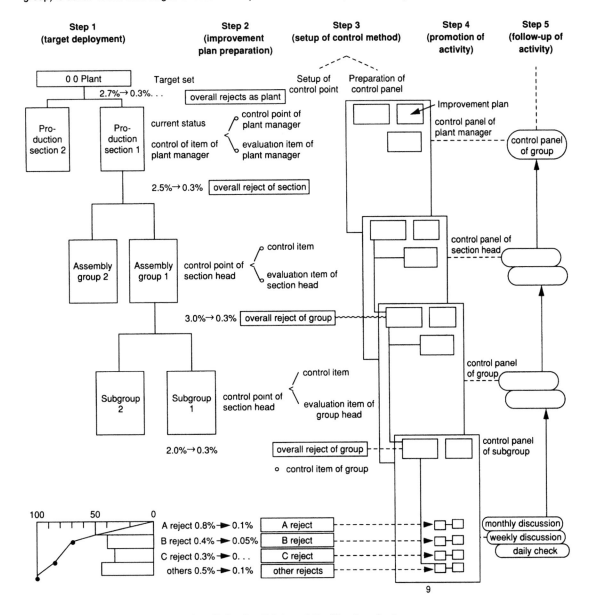

Figure 3-5. Outline of Operation Zelcoba (Matsushita Electronics)

Operation Zelcoba

Zelcoba is the name of the Keyaki tree, whose shape is similar to that of a policy plan within an organization. The purpose of this operation is to reduce rejects in the production process. The basic concept can be stated as follows:

- If the process is not straight-flow, it is considered to be worthless.
- The target is 0.3 percent.
- All products and all lines are subjects.
- All supervisors are leaders.
- Voluntary involvement of QC circles is necessary.

The point of this operation is to deploy a target — that is, a 0.3 percent rejection rate for each position (plant manager, section head, group head) — the achievement of which each position controls. The steps are as follows:

Step 1: Deploy the Target

Set the target for each reject item, machine, line, and operator according to the current situation.

Step 2: Prepare an Improvement Plan

Each position prepares an improvement plan to achieve the target for each business term. They display it on a control panel for control.

Step 3. Determine the Control Method

Each position determines a target achievement control point and displays it on the control panel.

Step 4: Promote Activities for Reducing Production Process Rejects

The plant manager heads the improvement effort, documenting progress in each department and work station.

Step 5: Initiate Follow-up Activities

Each position follows up on improvement activities, tracks progress toward achievement of the target, and studies methods to improve delays. Meanwhile, the plant managers and section heads offer specific instructions and motivation.

The control panel used in this deployment of the target-means is similar to the one shown in Figure 3-6. This figure is for the jobs in the section and group. Here, only a monthly graph is shown, but the control panel for the subgroup consists of daily graphs. The work sheet attached to each control panel is formalized.

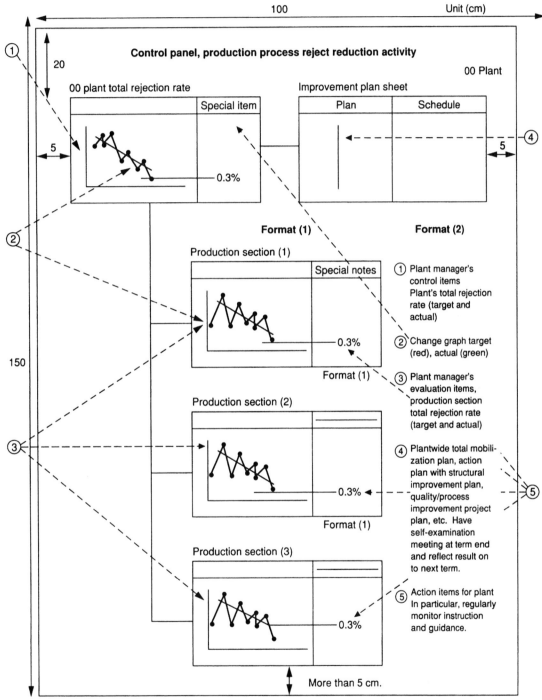

Note: This figure shows the points of explanation of this chapter added to the figure of p.645 of
"Companywide QC" by K. Ishihara (1984)

Figure 3-6. Control Panel (Matsushita Electronics)

Coordinating the Target-Means and Control Items

An important feature of policy deployment is coordination among all levels at the planning (setup stage) for the target-means. This assures uniformity of methods used, a common understanding of upper-level policy, and participation by lower levels.

Figure 3-7 outlines a policy deployment used at Ricoh (S. Tokiwa 1979). It resembles a typical company business plan system but is distinguished by the coordination at each stage. The steps for the deployment of the annual policy are described below.

Planned Policy, Coordination, Determination

Policy Planning by the President and the Business Department Head

Problems remaining from the previous term and new problems are addressed in the president's annual policy. The results are published at an annual management strategy meeting, together with the medium-term vision. Department policy is planned accordingly.

The business department policy focuses on issues such as performance, targets, priority plans, and structural improvement plans. It is determined after consultation with top managers on the appropriateness of the targets and specific progress made toward those ends. The department head sets the control items for checking the priority items so that they do not end up as mere slogans. Priority items can be divided into control items and request items, as shown in Figure 3-8.

Control Items for the Division Head

Control items are expressed as characteristic values — that is, Q (quality), C (cost), and D (quantity, delivery) — of the project; they clarify the resources invested and the method of control. A priority plan is presented at the policy presentation meeting twice a year. This is usually attended by management at levels higher than the group heads of the division. At the same time, the specific plan and the manner of promoting it are explained by the head of each related department.

Policy Planning by the Department Head

After getting the policy from the division head, the department head plans a policy that reflects problems that remain from the previous term, as well as

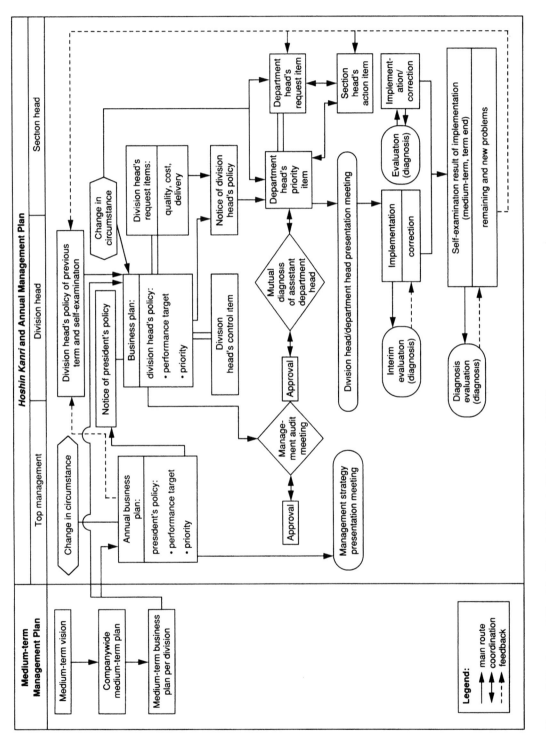

Figure 3-7. Annual *Hoshin Kanri* at Ricoh (S. Tokiwa 1979)

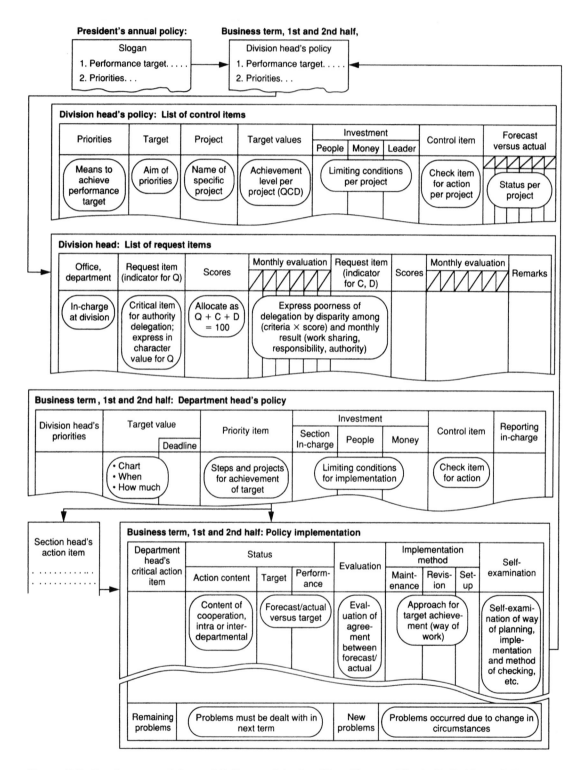

Figure 3-8. Deployment of Annual Policy and Action Plan Chart at Ricoh (S. Tokiwa 1979)

new problems. He or she consults with section heads as they tailor the policy to each section.

Coordination between Division and Department Heads

The division heads meet with various department heads to solve problems in interdepartmental relations and to link activities to related departments. Finally, they approve and determine the policy for the department.

Coordination between Department and Assistant Department Heads

Department and assistant department heads hold a brainstorming session to discuss problems and propose corrective actions. They reach a consensus about commonly shared problems based on the production policy presented.

Determining the Action Items for the Section Head

After receiving the policy from the department head, the section head makes an action plan and coordinates it with other section heads. Each then submits an action plan to the department head for approval.

A Meeting to Explain Department Policy

Twice a year, the department head holds policy explanation meetings in order to enhance understanding of the policy among workers in the sections.

Implementing the Policy

Each job position begins with a specific implementation action based on the policy and the implementation plan.

Evaluating the Progress of Implementation

An evaluation of implementation actions not only measures the extent to which the policy has been implemented but also strengthens human resources. The latter advantage is gained when evaluation results are used to coordinate actions among all job categories and to improve the capability of the managers. The evaluation process can be explained as follows.

1. Subject:
   - Difference between the targeted and actual results (results, targets)
   - The process by which the target was achieved (process, cause, means)

2. Purpose:
   - To ensure achievement of the policy (target-means)
   - To revise the plan and its implementation according to circumstances
   - To direct and guide the improvement effort

3. Method:
   - A status report of the implementation is prepared and submitted to the sub-commission (at mid-term and end of term)
   - Upper job positions can assess the reports and make decisions

Deployment of the Target-Means and Control Items

A method has been proposed in Chapter 1 by which to study the strengths of the relationships between target deployments and means, the target-means matrix that was first applied at Kobayashi Kosei (Figure 1-2). This is especially effective when you want to clarify the relationship between multiple targets and multiple means. One feature is the designation of a record number, control items, and control information for each target-means at the setup stage of the target-means for policy deployment. An outline of this is given in Figure 3-9. This can be further deployed to the division head, department head, and section head, as shown in Figure 3-10. This is all built into the matrix.

Hoshin Kanri and the Seven New QC Tools

The seven QC tools are effective for handling data. The QC methods development group at JUSE, headed by Nayatani, has proposed using the seven *new* QC tools as a QC method for thought processes. The seven new QC tools are the

1. Relationship chart
2. Affinity chart
3. System chart
4. Matrix
5. Matrix data analysis
6. PDPC (process determination plan, major failure-forecast chart)
7. Arrow diagram

Further, Nayatani has proposed using the seven new QC tools in policy deployment. An outline of the system in which the seven new QC tools are incor-

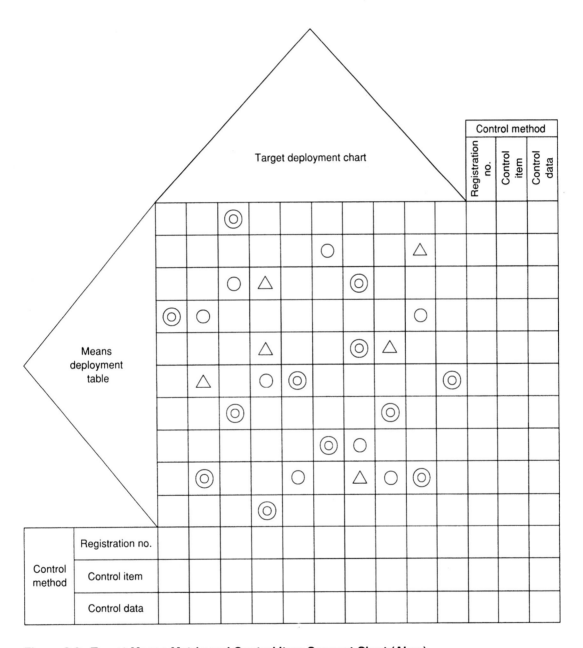

Figure 3-9. Target-Means Matrix and Control Item Concept Chart (Akao)

porated is shown in Table 3-2. Here, the seven new QC tools are used in various studies to analyze problems, proposals, opinions, and measures. The target-means system chart for setting the control items, the arrow diagram for control, the PDPC schedule chart, and other matrix charts are effective as control tools.

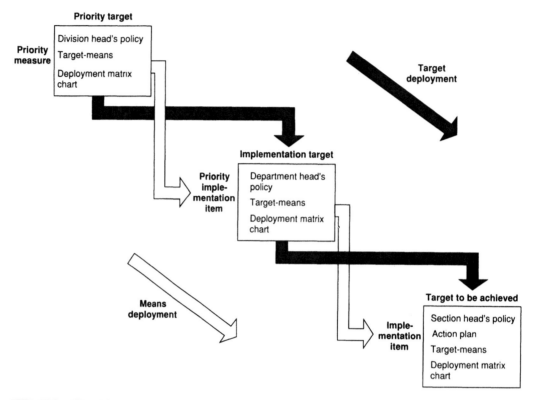

Figure 3-10. Target-Means Matrix from Target and Means Deployments (Kobayashi Kosei)

Target deployment

Target deployment table		
Division head's priority target	**Department head's action target**	**Team section achievement target**

Division head's priority target:
No. Q1 | reduction of product claims | less than 000 cases

Department head's action target:
No.
Q1K | production section 1 | less than 00 cases
Q1R | production department 2 | less than 00 cases

Team section achievement target:
No.
Q1K1 | production section 1 | less than xx cases
Q1K1 | production section 2 | less than xx cases
Q1K3 | QC section | less than xx cases

Production department 1, action target and department section action item, matrix chart

			QA				Education			
		Department's action item	Q1K	Q2K	Q3K	11	E2K	Regis-tration number	Control item	Control data
Priority action item	No.	Department section action team	reduction of product claims to less than 00 cases	major claim of priorty new products: 0 cases	major accidents of priority new products: 0 cases	reduction of lock-out rate	QC method utilization cases, 0000 cases/yr.			
1-1 Arrangement for new product introduction	1-1-1	study of reliability test and storage sample	◎	○	○	○		K1119	improve-ment status	P-A chart
	1-1-2	market quality, review and improvement of information system at initial fluid stage	◎	○	○	○		K1129		
	1-1-3	arrangement of new product failure history control system	○	○	○	○		K1133		
8-1 Activation of QC circle	8-1-1	full use of QC circle manual	○	○	○	○	○	K811W	# of themes completed	control graph
Registration No.			Q1K9	Q2K9	Q3K9	11K9	E2K9			
control item			No. of claims	new product	major claim	lock-out	use of QC meth.			

Table 3-2. *Hoshin Kanri* and Use of Seven New QC Tools (Nayatani)

Steps	Possible Use of Seven New QC Tools	Remarks
1. Planning of medium- and long-term policy	Affinity chart, target-means relation chart, problem/cause relation chart, target-means system chart, affinity chart for departmental discussion, relation chart, summary of system chart, matrix chart of top management vision and departmental proposal	The author has summarized and added the explanations and descriptions of the tools used in the examples, taking into consideration what has been written in the original books.
2. Decision on this year's president's policy	Target-means relation chart or target-means system chart, task collection affinity chart, target-means relation chart per task or target-means system chart, functional problem collection affinity chart, functional divisional task collection matrix, difference analysis priority item or problem/factor relation chart, functional target-means relation chart or system chart, management target-means matrix	
3. Deployment to departments • Setup and deployment of target • Problem for target achievement • Determine action measures (major item) • Detail deployment of each action measure (major item) • Measure (major item) and detailed deployment are evaluated and contents of final action are arranged • Arrange sequentially the detailed deployments of each measure • Summarize division policy and department policy	Target deployment by system chart, problem/factor relation chart for analysis of inhibitive factors against target achievement, target-means major item relation chart, various problem-factor matrix, engineering improvement history PDPC, medium- and long-term forecast problem-means affinity chart, action measure (major item) detail of deployment system chart, and higher dimension deployment system chart, arrow diagram type schedule plan (in case of high degree of uncertainty), division head's policy – departmental policy matrix, division target – policy matrix, president's policy – division policy compatibility matrix	
4. Implementation of policy and dept. policy • Audit/self-inspection of setup of annual policy • Implement policy • Review and change of policy at interim period • Study of performance of companywide and each department at end of term	Control item of target (result) and that of means (factor) and check with arrow diagram type of PDPC schedule, rewriting of PDPC (go to steps 1 and 2 after management's top audit diagnosis)	

Various methods have been developed to promote policy deployment. For example, the Comany Company has the hoshin seven tools as one feature of its policy deployment system. These are the

1. Corrective measure proposal
2. Target-means deployment chart
3. Priority action plan
4. Control graph
5. Anomaly report
6. QC story sheet
7. Policy deployment evaluation chart

At Comany, understanding of the policy is enhanced by the practice in which each employee checks himself by using the employees' manual, another feature of the system. The hoshin manual standardizes the use of the seven tools and provides education in order to promote the policy deployment process.

Here, the PDCA is used, the QC story sheet for the policy deployment results are checked using the hoshin evaluation sheet, coordination is done through a proposal sheet or a target-means deployment chart, and the check and anomaly report use control graphs and other tools.

Method of Determining and Using the Control Items

The Policy Deployment Control Item Setup Procedure

Deployment of the policy (target and means) generally proceeds as follows.

Step 1: Use a CA Chart to Check the Previous Year's Results

The check action table is the same as Table 2-5 in Chapter 2. First, you analyze the performance for this year, assessing the degree to which the target was achieved and listing any problems. Then you analyze the causes of each problem through a fishbone diagram. Next, you confirm the effects of the causes through a Pareto analysis of the data, looking at factors such as the amount of defects or the rate of defect. Once you discover a critical cause, you list the means for expected results, clarify a control purpose, and check it against the policy of your supervisor.

Step 2: Study the Results of the CA Check and Prepare a Target-Means Matrix

The control purpose of the CA table becomes the target item (control characteristic), and a target value and prioritized measures are derived from the expected results and conceived measures, respectively. The target-means is set up on the basis of the concepts shown in Figure 3-11.

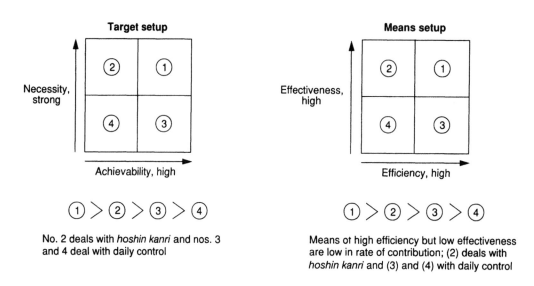

Figure 3-11. Concept of Setup of Target and Means

1. The target is set up from two aspects: necessity and achievability. Necessity takes priority. For example, a target of being in the black must be created when a company is in the red. When the anti-pollution laws were enacted, the auto industry declared it impossible to develop an engine that would satisfy all the requirements. Nevertheless, the decision had been made and auto manufacturers rose to the challenge.
2. Means (priority action items) are determined from two aspects: effectiveness and efficiency. Effectiveness always takes priority.
3. Necessity and effectiveness depend on the capability of each person, but they also need to be based on data (control items).

Kano uses yardsticks to measure the purpose and efficiency of control items.

• *The purpose yardstick:* This is related to the main purpose of the work and always relates to the output of the department involved. Here, work includes both daily work under daily control and special assignments deployed from policy.

- *The efficiency yardstick:* This measures how efficiently work is done in the department involved and is related to the productivity yardstick.

Priority should be placed on the purpose yardstick, of course. Kano cites examples in which efficiency yardsticks are placed ahead of purpose yardsticks in his QC diagnosis.

Nayatani (1978) proposes a concept whereby the control item of the target is that of the result system (control point) and the control item of the means is that of the factor system for achieving the target (checkpoint). When the two concepts are joined, then the control item for the target is from the result system and purpose yardstick. The control item of the means is from the factor system and the efficiency or the purpose yardstick, depending on the job category and means. Akao recommends checking the progress status by using a schedule (one kind of checkpoint) without setting up a formal checkpoint. This works well when the checkpoint is difficult to find in relation to the means. Another device is the check sheet shown in Figure 3-12.

Step 3: Prepare the Individual Action Plans

Prepare an individual action plan (also called a hoshin action status sheet) for each priority item. It should list control purposes and control items (control points and checkpoints). Use a control graph to check progress toward target against the action plan. For targets, use the control graph (control chart, etc.); for means, use the control graph, number table, report, schedule control (arrow diagram, PERT, Gantt chart), control sheet, drawings (for example, a map of the sales area), and other tools.

Step 4. Prepare the Control Item Network and List Control Items

Control item networks are used to clarify the arrangements of inter-job category control items, to link control items from daily control and that of policy deployment, and to check for duplication. An example is shown in Figure 3-13. Here, the relationship among control items for the department head and section heads is shown (control point: CL; checkpoint: CK). In this division there are three types of department-head control items, five department-head checkpoints, 44 section-head control points, and 25 section-worker control points. The checkpoints of a supervisor sometimes serve as control points for subordinates. Table 3-3 shows these types in its list of control items.

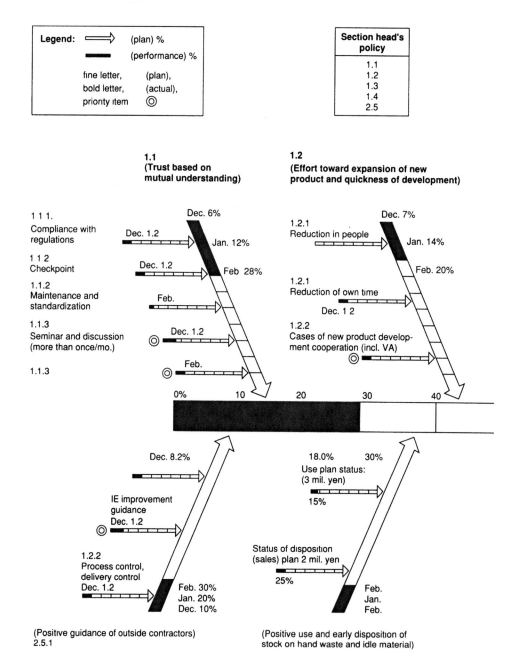

Figure 3-12. Plan Status Check Sheet (Warehouse Group)

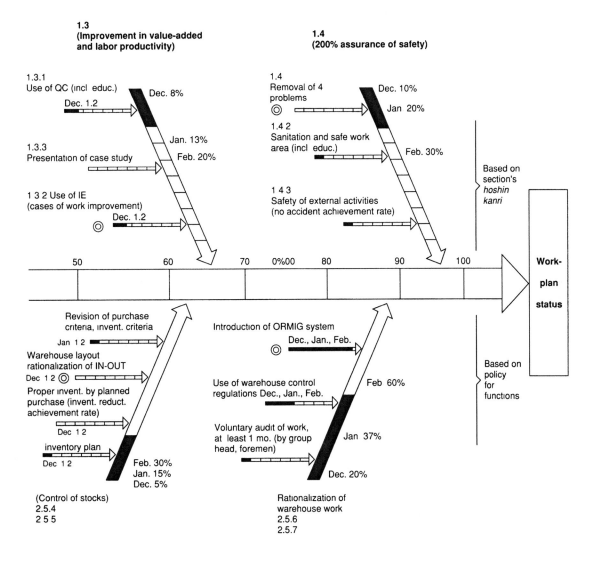

1.3
(Improvement in value-added and labor productivity)

1.3.1
Use of QC (incl educ.)
Dec. 1.2   Dec. 8%

1.3.3
Presentation of case study   Jan. 13%
                                          Feb. 20%

1 3 2 Use of IE
(cases of work improvement)
              Dec. 1.2

1.4
(200% assurance of safety)

1.4
Removal of 4   Dec. 10%
problems
                      Jan 20%

1.4 2
Sanitation and safe work
area (incl educ.)   Feb. 30%

1 4 3
Safety of external activities
(no accident achievement rate)

50   60   70   0%00   80   90   100

Work-
plan
status

Based on
section's
*hoshin
kanri*

Based on
policy
for
functions

Revision of purchase
criteria, invent. criteria
Jan 1 2

Warehouse layout
rationalization of IN-OUT
Dec 1 2
Proper invent. by planned
purchase (invent. reduct.
achievement rate)
Dec 1 2

inventory plan
Dec 1 2   Feb. 30%
                           Jan. 15%
                           Dec. 5%

(Control of stocks)
2.5.4
2 5 5

Introduction of ORMIG system
              Dec., Jan., Feb.

Use of warehouse control
regulations Dec., Jan., Feb.   Feb 60%

Voluntary audit of work,
at least 1 mo. (by group   Jan 37%
head, foremen)

                           Dec. 20%

Rationalization of
warehouse work
2.5.6
2.5.7

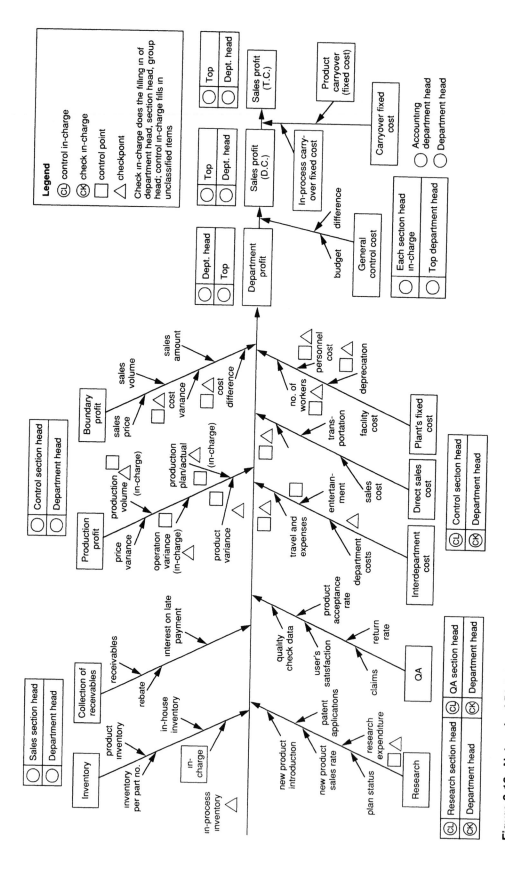

Figure 3-13. Network of Division Work Control Items

Table 3-3. List of Control Items (Form Example)

								Stamps	
								Depart-ment	Section head
Job Category	**Job Title and Contents**					**Preparation Date**			
						Review date			
Unit work	Control item	Reg. No.	Criticality			Check, date				Control level, target and control limit	Anomaly handling	Control data	Related standards	
			A	B	C	yr.	per	mo.	day					

Points of Caution for Determining Control Items

Control Point

You use a control point at the check stage of a control cycle. This enables you to do the following:

- Provide a yardstick (measure) to measure the results
- Determine the methods by which actions will be performed and establish the judgment criteria (control level)
- Decide the handling methods, responsibilities, authority, and reporting in cases of emergency
- Determine the frequency of checking (by hour, shift, day, week, month, year)
- Review control points regularly

Checkpoint

Use the checkpoints to verify the factors at the implementation stage of the plan in the control cycle.

- Determine the cause (factor) for prevention.
- Determine items for adjustment, arrangement, and confirmation based on these.
- Determine priorities so that things can change over time.

- Have each section worker or supervisor select them.
- Control points for lower job categories can derive from the check items of the upper managers. Although authority can be delegated, responsibility remains with the supervisor.

Using Control Items

Separate the Use of Control Points and Checkpoints

Generally, checkpoints are checked by the lower-level managers and are left alone by upper-level managers. Although the points are prioritized, they may differ depending on policy and priorities.

Checkpoints are checked against results, so they have certain values and judgment criteria (target value, plan line, control limit line). Therefore, use of control charts, control graphs, and numerical tables is effective for graphic control.

A checkpoint is a "check of the factor" or a "control of the process"; factor circumstances (society or economy) affecting control points must also be checked. Thus, a check by control should always involve checkpoints. These can also be used to instruct and to motivate workers as evaluation items. There are three controls: a pre-control, a fact control, and a post-control.

- *Pre-controls* are used to prevent the cause. Here, forecasting and warnings can be prepared to control in advance. For example, political risk analysis (Figure 3-14) and profit calculations for investments in facilities and equipment can use pre-control. In this type of control, process analysis and target and plan setups are essential, as is a well-established technology. This is to prevent critical defects or failures that require special knowledge of processes. It is better to apply this to only the most important items, using a Pareto system.
- *Fact control* is controlling at the "do" stage, while things such as work check are in progress. Often adjustments or checks and repairs result from this control. Upper and middle managers tend to favor this type of control. The cost of fact control is normally low, but should an accident occur, it can be very high. Thus, feedback of information and communication is vital.

    When control items are selected for policy deployment, pre-control items are for checking both the long-term or the short-term at the planning stage and for deploying the policy. Fact control is used mostly for checkpoints; action is taken by delegating authority or voluntarily. Fact control is applied to the "trivial many" in a Pareto manner.

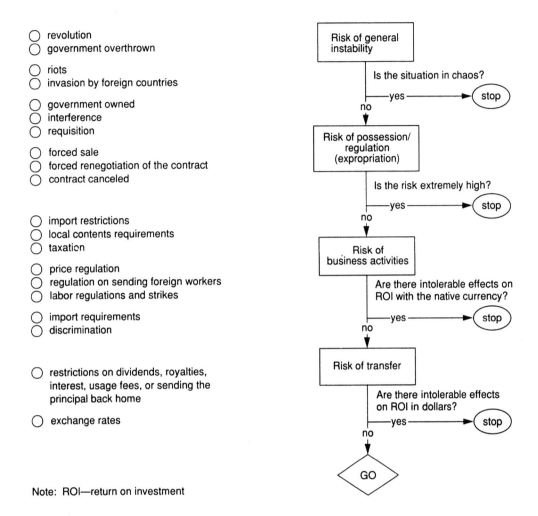

○ revolution
○ government overthrown

○ riots
○ invasion by foreign countries

○ government owned
○ interference
○ requisition

○ forced sale
○ forced renegotiation of the contract
○ contract canceled

○ import restrictions
○ local contents requirements
○ taxation

○ price regulation
○ regulation on sending foreign workers
○ labor regulations and strikes

○ import requirements
○ discrimination

○ restrictions on dividends, royalties, interest, usage fees, or sending the principal back home

○ exchange rates

Risk of general instability

Is the situation in chaos?
——yes——→ stop
no

Risk of possession/ regulation (expropriation)

Is the risk extremely high?
——yes——→ stop
no

Risk of business activities

Are there intolerable effects on ROI with the native currency?
——yes——→ stop
no

Risk of transfer

Are there intolerable effects on ROI in dollars?
——yes——→ stop
no

GO

Note: ROI—return on investment

Figure 3-14. Evaluation of Political Risks in the Decision-making Process for Overseas Investment

- *Post-control* is used to check the results after the "do" stage. This is control with the use of information. Performance evaluations at the end of a term regarding the status of rejects, failures, anomalies, or targets are suitable for this. Fact control can include yardsticks or schedules for checkpoints of the means, the level of achievement of each event in a PERT, and so on. Evaluation for post-control is not expressed in numbers. Rather, items such as evaluations of targets and performances are used.

These types of control must be selected properly. Generally, upper management is more in charge of the pre- and post-controls, while lower levels use fact control.

Control Item "Duds"

Some companies have discontinued use of control graphs and control charts because "control items are useless." Figure 3-15 shows this "dull period." A negative attitude about control items will ensure that they end up as "firecracker duds." It is important to build "live" control items. Then a set number of control items, and thus a control system, can be established.

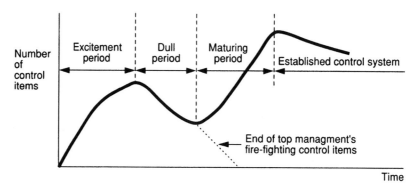

Figure 3-15. Change in Number of Control Items

Proper Use of Control Items

To prevent control items from turning into "duds," keep the following points in mind:

- Everybody involved should participate when the control items are set up.
- Staff members should act as a warning system and submit suggestions as soon as anomalies are discovered.
- Once an anomaly is discovered, take action right away.
- Develop methods for using the control items on a continuing basis.
- Make sure control items are devised so as to lighten the work load.
- Get a taste for control items as soon as possible.

Control Items and QC Technique

Because they deal with data, control items are often applied to quantifiable things, such as targets. QC techniques are helpful in this respect. Table 3-4 is an application example of QC techniques for control items in management control.

Table 3-5 shows examples of QC techniques used for QC items in sales QC activities. Often, the seven QC tools are used, but recently more advanced methods have been used as well.

Table 3-4. Relation between Control Items and QC Techniques for Management Control

Control Items	Control Tools	Types of QC Techniques
Total capital profit rate, sales profit	Fishbone diagram for total profit, fishbone diagram for sales profit	Fishbone diagram
Profitability index, sales amount (monthly, accumulated, 12-month movement), sales amount, collection amount	Radar chart for profitability, Z (L) chart for sales control, control chart (flow curves)	Graphs
Financial indicator	Financial indicator scoring	Histogram
Volume variance Rate of variance in cost	Control chart for volumetric variance and change rate	Control chart
Sales amount, profit (rate) Value-added productivity, production cost	Capability chart for processes	Process capability index
Break-even point, sales amount, profit, salary, work classification pay	Break-even chart, profit chart, job classification pay conversion	Relation/regression

Table 3-5. Activity Items of Sales, Control Items, and QC Techniques

Action Item	Control Item	Analysis Tools and Techniques
Sales control	Sales amount, price change rate, order intake change rate, sales cost	Achievement of target, price, order intake changes, sales cost – fishbone diagram, Pareto chart
Sales expansion	Sales expansion rate, demand, frequency of visits, sales inventory	Fishbone diagram, inactive product, Pareto chart per factor, share expansion analysis, functional analysis
Sales efficiency improvement	Returns rate, inventory days, collection site, sales per person, profit per person, delivery improvement: no. of days	Cost of product, returns, inventory character chart, Pareto analysis, sales ranking, returns, matrix, pattern analysis
Claim handling	No. of days for handling, no. of claims per unit sales amount	Fishbone diagram, Pareto analysis per each factor (in-house and at outside)
New product development	New product sales rate	Fishbone diagram of low activity product, graph
Collection of quality information	No. of effective days/case (effective cases/total cases)	Preparation of quality information collection procedure sheet

The Concept of Control Levels

The concept of the control item is based on the control cycle, the fishbone diagram, and the control chart. The specific tasks involved include checking the PDCA cycle, checking causes, checking results, judging criteria for anomalies, setting control limit lines, and handling limit lines. Judgment criteria (for example, control levels) are the results of applying the concept of control charts to the features of handling data. A control level is expressed as a control line — that is, a median line and the control limit lines that you determine by analyzing data. For control items in policy deployment, the target value, or target line, is determined by target deployment. The handling limit line determines nonachievement of the target and indicates action to be taken on the cause of that nonachievement. In other words, when the handling limit line is crossed, action must be taken (Figure 3-16 (3). In means deployment, the control level is based on the checkpoints. But here, each completion date for the events — that is, the schedule, delivery, or PERT, of the work progress control chart — and the degree to which the means were achieved correspond to control levels.

The control level of the control point uses a control graph and control chart. Generally, you apply targets to *hoshin kanri* (improvement) and control charts to daily control (maintenance). In Figure 3-16, for example, there are four types of control levels:

1. Target-policy line
2. Actual level
3. Technical-statistical level
4. Market level

The pluses and minuses of these types are listed in Table 3-6.

How to Determine Control Levels

Target-policy Line

Sales targets or production targets for the end of term are examples of target-policy lines (Figure 3-16[1]). A Z or L chart can be used. Upper action (control) limits (UCL) and lower action (control) limits (LCL) are obtained from past performances of 62 sales offices in the company and based on 10-day and 20-day histograms. For the first five days of a month, achievement can be as low as 50 per-

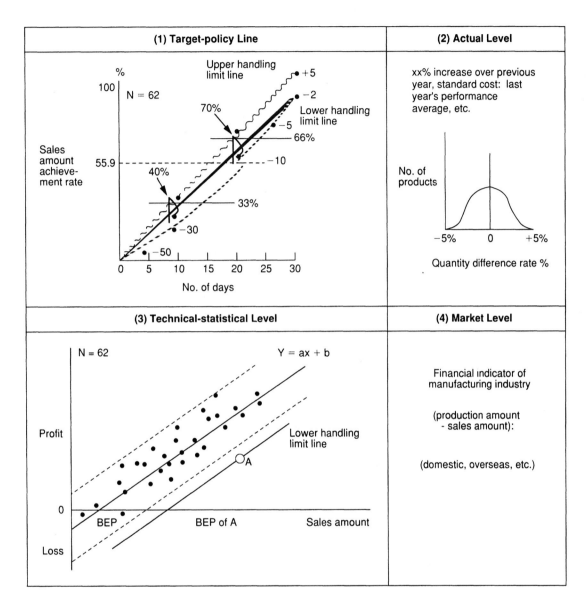

Figure 3-16. Control Level for Control Point

cent, but if it is 10 percent short of completion on the 20th day, then the completion rate can fail from 100 percent. Recovery in the last 10 days is difficult if the histogram for 20 days does not show a 66 percent average, 70 percent maximum, 55.9 percent minimum. Set by policy on the basis of experience are plus 5 percent and minus 2 percent.

Table 3-6. Advantages and Disadvantages of Four Control Level Types

Type	Advantage	Disadvantage
Target-policy line	• Specific expression of management stance • Motivation of subordinates	• Statistical dispersion can be amiss • Often changed or corrected
Actual level	• Strong explanation to businesspeople • Good standard achievement, compatibility, stability, and fairness	• Poor performance can become permanent • Hard to enhance spirit for breakthrough
Technical-statistical level	• Tells how it should be technically • No blindness to true feasibility, which is inherent to historical level • Statistical level has anomaly judgment criteria	• Way of control level with technical accuracy of management function is not there yet • Control level's conditions of achievability, compatibility, fairness, and economy are not satisfied
Market level	• Market data is useful; company that has it expands • Good indication of competitiveness	• For quality function, it is not mature yet • What is market must be defined

Actual Level

To determine actual level (Figure 3-16[2]), you set a target value such as XX percent increase over last year. The standard cost is normally based on last year's actual average. When the action limit was set up for this three-sigma limit, it was approximately 5 percent from the histogram of quantitative difference rates for all products.

Technical-statistical Levels

A sales target is like a theoretical yield in the chemical industry. A straight rate equal to 100 percent is one of these. Typical statistical levels are control lines of control charts in which the calculation formula is clear. Figure 3-16(3) shows the variance (relation) chart of the sales profit and loss in the 62 sales offices. An average companywide break-even point (BEP) can be obtained by drawing a straight regression line, and a three-sigma line approximating the regression analysis can be used as the UCL and LCL. For example, sales office A has good sales and profits, but its BEP is outside of the company's LCL and its profit is low in relation to its sales amounts. That is, its fixed costs are high.

Market Level

A company often uses financial data and industrial indicators to judge its position in the market. Information of this sort can be purchased from market research companies.

Revision/Deletion

A control level can be revised or deleted in response to the following circumstances:

- Policy change
- Long-term control condition
- Change in control level due to improvements or breakthroughs
- Changes in society, economy, or industry
- Acts of nature
- Normal changes

CHAPTER 4

Hoshin Kanri with Daily Control, Cross-functional Management, and Work Plans

Hoshin Kanri and Daily Control

The proportion of daily control to hoshin activities varies, but generally 75 to 95 percent is daily control and 5 to 25 percent is hoshin. This is because daily control is the base and policy deployment is effective only when daily control is performed correctly. Both systems grew out of TQC, and they are used in combination for implementing business and management plans. Daily control is used to maintain and control the current control level, whereas policy deployment is used to improve the current control level. Exemplifying the concept that "control and improvement are the two wheels of a vehicle," daily control and policy deployment can be classified as control activities and improvement activities, respectively. Figure 4-1 illustrates this concept. The area shown in dotted lines is control of the European or American type. It differs from the Japanese type in that improvement is pushed during daily control and setup is effected through improvement breakthroughs. The difference between it and continual improvement through policy deployment and daily control is important. K. Ishikawa noted this at the Dainippon Ink Company's fifth QC circle seminar, held in March 1988. Policy deployment is a problem-solving activity used to assign priorities to management

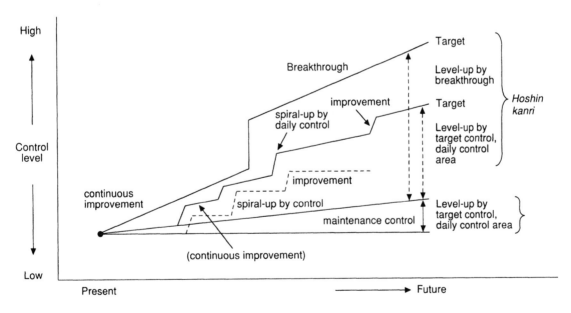

Note: K. Hirose (1986), Quality Control Monthly Text, "QC Circle Activity and *Hoshin kanri* for Sales-Service Industries," p. 57, Fig. 13, Quality Monthly Committee, is the basis of this chart.

Figure 4-1. Difference between *Hoshin Kanri* and Daily Control

tasks. Daily control can be called routine work activity. But both of these are performed simultaneously at each department or section. The results of improvement through policy deployment are built into daily control activities through prevention, standardization of steps, and the QC story. Thus, the cycle of daily control can be called the SDCA cycle, that is, standardization-do-check-action. Critical problems checked during the SDCA cycle in daily control are then taken up by policy deployment tasks. Figure 4-2 shows the control steps of daily control and the QC story in policy deployment. The control steps are the movement from the PDCA cycle to the SDCA cycle or vice versa.

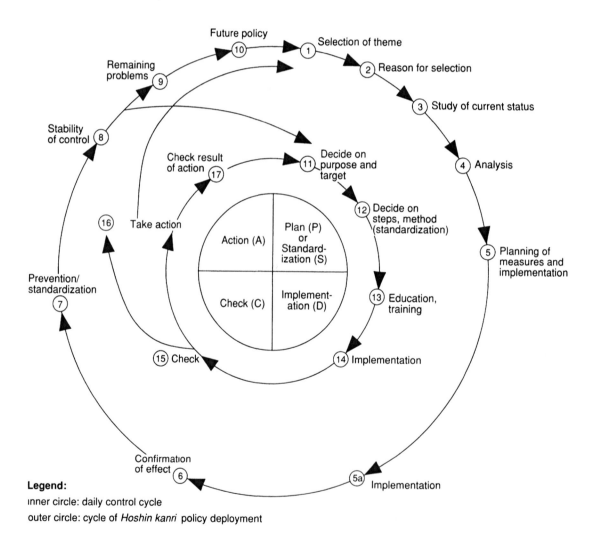

Legend:
inner circle: daily control cycle
outer circle: cycle of *Hoshin kanri* policy deployment

Figure 4-2. Mutual Movement of Control (Daily Control) and Improvement (*Hoshin Kanri*) Activity

Integration of Daily Control and *Hoshin Kanri* through Control Items

Some time ago, Akao pointed out the existence of control items for improvement and for maintenance. Later he matched them with hoshin control and daily control. This concept is shown in Figure 4-3. Kano (1983) classified these categories further:

1. Control items contained only in daily control
2. Control items contained within hoshin control and daily control
3. Control items contained only in hoshin control

He made them into a list of control items for implementation of policy deployment and daily control without separating the two types of activity. He has shown an example of "work deployment" and policy deployment at Tokyo Juki Kogyo Company. Kobayashi Kosei also uses the "job study table" (Table 4-1) to clarify work contents and for work deployment, prepared control item network, added control item setup through a target-means matrix, summarized control items through policy deployment, and daily control. Table 4-2 is a prepared list of the controlled items. You can think of this as a means of "interfacing the controlled items."

In interfacing these control items you must determine a classification by mutually checking the work deployed, as Kano proposed, with action items for the policy. One method of mutually checking the control items might work as follows (Figure 4-4). A work function system chart is prepared with the help of Ishihara's method for work deployment, and control items are set up for each job (here, it is to the fourth level). Meanwhile, control items from target control are made into a matrix and a control item relation matrix is prepared; a mutual check will determine classification. Items outside the control item relation matrix usually have no deployment items. Here, control items of hoshin control and daily control are only classified; inside this column, the mutual relationship is classified. A circle symbol marks cases where there is a relationship but no agreement. The effectiveness and convenience of this method has yet to be studied.

Means/Business Plan Matrix

Akao has proposed a plan whereby the means of improving the present control system for implementing work plans (sales, production, facility, etc.) can be implemented regardless of policy deployment. The aims are to integrate work and TQC and to improve the effects of arrangements on the work plan.

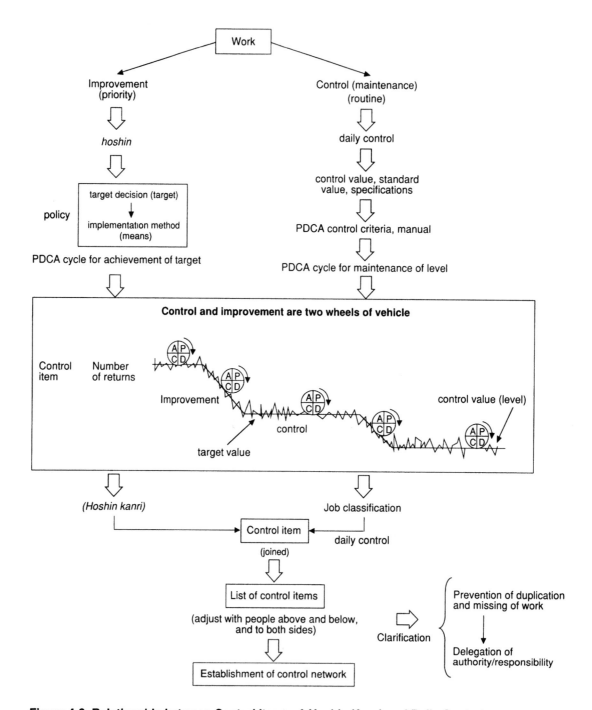

Figure 4-3. Relationship between Control Items of *Hoshin Kanri* and Daily Control

Table 4-1. Job Study Table (Kobayashi Kosei)

Present job work (per function)	Purpose of work	Judgment data	Judgment criteria	Handling method	Related data

Hoshin Kanri and Cross-functional Management

Along with policy deployment, cross-functional management plays a major role in TQM promotion. Overall control of QCD (quality, cost, delivery), the indispensable conditions for TQM, cannot be achieved without cross-functional management. Professor Ishikawa of Musashi Kogyo University explained cross-functional management in 1960 by preparing a chart of departmental and functional elements for an organization he modeled on cloth (made up of the warp and the woof). He emphasized the importance of cross-functional communication in organizations. This, it may be remembered, was in a strictly hierarchical society that emphasized departments.

Since then, many industries have adopted the concept of cross-functional management; the example of Toyota Motors (Figure 2-13) has already been cited. This was made in 1981, after a trial-and-error process that had begun in 1961. In addition to QCD, companies are also regarding as functions new product development, sales management, purchase management, safety management, personnel management, and information management. Normally, the senior manager in charge of a function is the chairperson, and directors of related departments are members of a functional committee (QA committee, cost control committee, production volume control committee, etc.). Responsibility for and authority of each function are assigned to each department, and the resulting actions of each department are assessed cross-functionally. When the system is planned, implemented, checked, and improved, the cross-departmental relationship is strengthened, creating a high efficiency management system. Thus, cross-functional management is a control-improvement activity through which management can plan companywide functional targets for setting up policy deployment and daily control in line departments and for ultimately checking and taking action on the

Table 4-2. List of Control Items (Kobayashi Kosei)

List of control items			Date prepared	
Area	Job	(Job name) Production section head of Kosei-brand products	Revision dates	10/15/79
production department 1 production section 2		(Job) Manager planned production volume according to finishing standards, most economically, and on time		1/12/80
				month day year

Basic work	Job	Daily control	Control item ○ (control point) △ (check point)	Cycle	Control level	Action	Data	Reg. No.
Q (quality) 1. Assure specification quality of Kosei-brand	1. Process control	*hoshin*	○ finishing process, reject rate	monthly	target, first 1/2 xx% (+0.3 %, −0.3%) 2nd 1/2 △△ $\triangle$ % (+0.3%, −0.3%)	cause analysis improvement instruction	process rejection rate control graph reject anomaly report	K 1262
	4. Improvement of process capability index (Cp)	*hoshin*	○ rate of Cp>1, major product	monthly	target 00%	cause analysis improvement instruction	rate of Cp>1, major product, control graph	K 12512

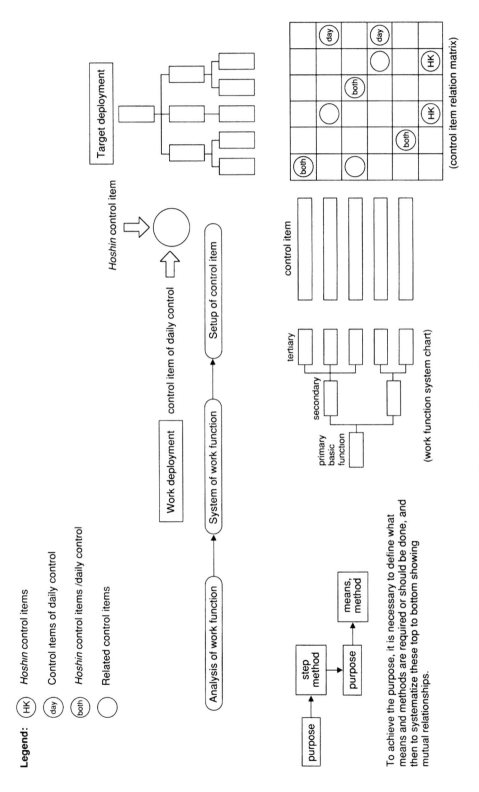

Figure 4-4. Joining of *Hoshin* Control Items and Daily Control (Draft Plan)

results. The relationship of policy deployment and daily control to departmental management, cross-functional management, and product control is detailed in Chapter 2. Product control requires departmental cooperation for both products and market development. Here, strategic business unit (SBU) teams perform activities for each product.

Cross-functional Policy and Departmental Policy

Production sales proceed on the basis of control by department, which itself is based on job line organizations. Higher management efficiency through cross-functional management is necessary. Top management benefits from a functional structure. Thus, important problems in cross-functional management are discussed at the functional committees and come out as functional policies. A functional policy is implemented and put under the control of the department that bears responsibility and authority. Therefore, cross-functional management needs to be built into the departmental policy at the policy setup stage. Functional policy must precede departmental policy. Toyota Auto Body uses an *X*-shaped matrix linking target and means for target-means deployment (Figure 4-5). In terms of control items, the upper portion of policy deployment in Figure 4-6 is preferable. Policy deployment and daily control are both summarized in the list of priority control items as control items for policy deployment (cross-functional management plus control by department). Control items for daily control are put into the list of job class control items and are classified through checks with the relationship matrix of the control items in the list of overall control items.

Thus, by linking hoshin and daily control, work in several job categories and departments is integrated and implemented. For cross-functional management, you report monthly on the status of the functional policy implementation for line departments to the functional department (functional committee office) in the form of a line department-cross-functional management report; the cross-functional department collects these and submits them to the cross-functional committee. Further, the cross-functional committee will contribute twice a year to the companywide cross-functional report. The president or a committee assesses the cross-functional control system. At Komatsu, a simultaneous check of control points in QA occurs at the same time.

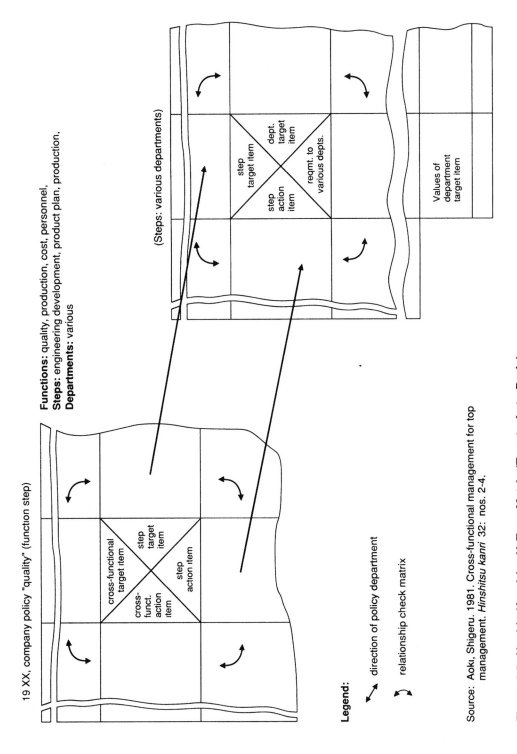

Figure 4-5. *Hoshin Kanri* by *X*-Type Matrix (Toyota Auto Body)

Source: Aoki, Shigeru. 1981. Cross-functional management for top management. *Hinshitsu kanri* 32: nos. 2-4.

Functions: quality, production, cost, personnel,
Steps: engineering development, product plan, production,
Departments: various

19 XX, company policy "quality" (function step)

(Steps: various departments)

cross-functional target item

cross-funct. action item

step target item

step action item

step target item

dept. target item

step action item

reqmt. to various depts.

Values of department target item

Legend:

↕ direction of policy department

↔ relationship check matrix

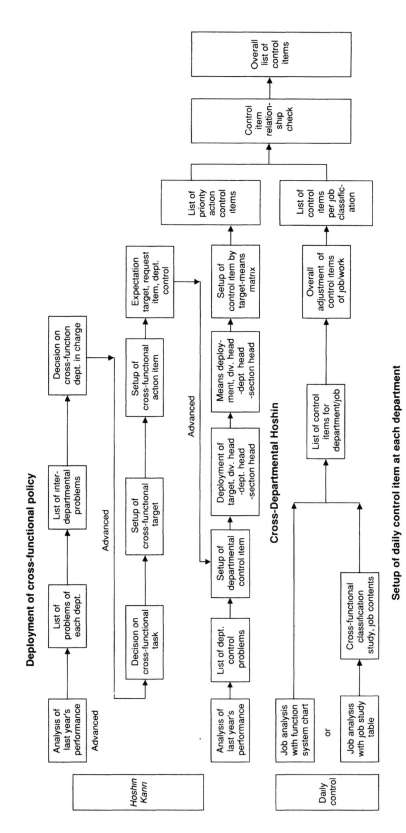

Figure 4-6. Integrating *Hoshin Kanri* and Daily Control by Control Item (Draft Plan)

Hoshin Kanri and Work Plans

Determining the target and means for policy deployment is of basic importance and can best be understood through study of the target-means matrix. One problem of policy deployment is its relationship to sales, production, and facility and equipment planning.

Work plans for these functions are implemented whether or not policy deployment or target control are in place. Budget control is implemented by making a sales plan and allocating a budget to each department. Market analysis is performed and medium- and long-term management plans made according to product strategy. Plans are prepared for sales, production, investment, personnel, R&D, and so on, and an annual policy is established. These are then deployed to each department, section, and group.

Sometimes these plans are treated as parallel action items in the action plan for policy deployment, or they can be implemented as separate work plans for daily control. At other times, important items in the work plan are included in the hoshin action plan sheet.

Table 4-3 is an action plan sheet (draft) of a target-means matrix for the production engineering section facility group of plant Y at company N. For example, item 2 — enhancement of the improvement action system — is for improving the system, but item 1 is the job that this facility group starts with. Improvement items of the system and action plans for work are often mixed in the action plan sheet.

When policy deployment is completely separated from the work plan, the question arises whether the work is separate from TQM. When there are many work improvement items, a lack of improvement of the system is underscored.

Merging *Hoshin Kanri* and the Work Plan

Achieving the work plan is essential to company management, but improving the system does not happen by itself. Therefore, the poorness of the process is clarified with the CA chart and the means-action item improved.

This improvement of the system should make it easier to implement the work plan as well. Work action items and improvement action items in the system (means) are listed in parallel positions at the top and bottom, as in Table 4-4. The purpose of each action item is clarified by the marks *(o)*, ◯, and Δ using a matrix with control purpose (control characteristic, control item, target characteristic). The *(o)*, ◯ and Δ indicate the degree of the contribution.

Improvement action items for this system are rotated as shown on the right-hand side of the table. In other words, the improvement action items for the system

Table 4-3. Example of Action Plan Sheet

Action plan sheet, 2d half-year 1984 (Production Engineering Facility Group)

No.	Action items (means)	Cost reduction (mill of yen)	Schedule compliance (%)	Facility reliability (more than %)	Opportunity loss (yen)	84/10	11	3
1.	Activity of project of OO	◎				Needs study, analysis (functional classification)	SHOP control function	System proposal sheet · production
(1)	Introduction, deployment of XXX system	○					current status, study and analysis	line machine no. 1 · system proposal
(2)	Development of automation and material handling line	◎						
(3)	Production △△ and CAM function	◎					CELL-DATA (Tree) qual. need in proc. · study needs analysis	production
(6)	Expansion of mass production line	◎			○			
2.	Enhancement of improvement action system	○	◎	◎	○		decision on method of administration	education guidance · how to draw charts
(1)	Deployment of activity (shorten supply schedule)	○	◎				review of priority facility	corrective action implementation
(2)	Promotion of 1984 activity	○	○	◎			collection of performance data · detailed plan	
(3)	Improvement of schedule plan accuracy		◎	◎	○			improvement of plan accuracy

Target value

control data:
- cost reduction control chart
- work control chart
- reliability control chart
- lost opportunity control chart

Table 4-4. Matrix of Means-Work

			2	1				
		Action Item	O O O O	× × × ×				
	Control purpose							
Means	1	▢▢▢▢	◎					
	2	∗ ∗ ∗ ∗		◎				
(improvement of arrangement)								
Work-plan	1	△△△△	◎					◎
	2	+ + + +		O				O
	Control character		· · ·	· · ·				
	Target value		· · ·	· · ·				

and the action items for the work are joined together in a matrix. The symbols *(o)*, ○, and Δ clarify the effects of the improvement action item for the system on the work action item. Regular action items are realized more effectively by this improvement of the system. Table 4-5 is an example of an improvement of Table 4-3 through use of the above method.

For example, once you perform a study of a facility, introducing evaluation criteria and establishing criteria, then you can introduce and deploy the XXX system

Table 4-5. Means-Work Matrix (Nippon Denki, Yamanashi Plant)

2d half-year, 1984, *Hoshin Kanri* action plan sheet (Production Engineering Facility Group)

Classification	No.	Action item	Plan schedule 1984	Plan schedule 11	Plan schedule 3
Improvement means	1	DR system and improvement	problem study		trial, evaluation
	2	design engineering enhancement	design engineering		manual arrangement
	3	maintenance improvement		priority control	manual arrangement
	4	introduction evaluation method and criteria	analysis of evaluation data		evaluation
	5	standardization	study of facility functional parts		plan
	6	review and improvement of investment evaluation method		problem point	trial, evaluation
	7	review of education for maintenance skill		individual skills	manual preparation
Work plan	1	introduction, deployment of XXX system	study needs		system proposal
	2	development/introduction of automatic parts feeder	analysis of current status		production
	3	development/introduction of material handling line		status check	measure
	4	prepare production data base	technical information check		manual
	5	expansion of OO CAM function		check needs	system proposal
	6	development/introduction △△ of SHOP control system	system report, system proposal		software production
	7	expansion of flow production line			production

Control purposes (No.):
1. facility reliability
2. downtime
3. investment
4. maintenance cost
5. delay in introduction
6. repair time

Conversion table / Control characteristics:

	1 facility reliability	2 MTBF	3 investment	4 maintenance cost	5 delayed introduction	6 MTTR
Control characteristics	facility reliability	MTBF	investment	maintenance cost	delayed introduction	MTTR
target value	<00%	HOO	100% ± 10%	100% ± 10%	<2 days	xxH/unit

and the YY shop control system without difficulty. The downward bending arrow in Table 4-5 shows the relationship between the improvement means and the work plan item.

In the past, the relationship between policy deployment and the work plan was not clearly understood; they were separated and later joined together. The merging of the two activities can serve as a hoshin action plan sheet.

This method for merging the improvement action items of the system emphasized in policy deployment and the work plan was an action plan sheet for one group only. It is important to analyze the current situation in your own company and to deploy annual policies and work plans that correspond to your particular needs.

CHAPTER 5

Implementation of *Hoshin Kanri*: Case Studies

CASE STUDY 1: *HOSHIN KANRI* AT AISIN-TAKAOKA

Aisin-Takaoka is a part of the Toyota automobile group and manufactures casting parts. It was established in 1960 at Toyota City in Aichi Pref. Currently, the goal of its quality management is to build a company based on the philosophy that quality is supreme and to become a core company within the Aisin group.

Aisin-Takaoka changed its name from Takaoka Kogyo on September 1, 1986, in order to enhance the total strength of the Aisin group and to improve the image of the company. *Hoshin kanri* at this company goes back to its founding, but not until TQC was introduced in 1977 did real control and administration begin.

The company introduced TQC in order to build a strong company structure that could withstand whatever environment it found itself in following the first oil crisis. In 1980 it won the Deming Prize, and in 1981, the Japan Quality Control Prize.

To assure its survival in severe operating conditions, the company makes the PDCA cycle and the spiral-up process of *hoshin kanri* important parts of its business management.

Management Strategy

Aisin-Takaoka's management philosophy is "creating a future in which quality is supreme." This is the basis of all its policies, management vision, and expectations for the company's future.

It has been 26 years since the company was founded, and its growth has not been smooth. In the first half of the 1980s, 80 percent of the company's products, casted auto parts, were jeopardized because of the two oil crises and export restrictions due to trade friction. The company also had to address the problems of the need for low fuel consumption, which resulted in lighter weight and more compact parts, and so it looked to develop other materials. Many meetings by the directors to deploy their "V plan" were meant to recover a performance that was heading downward. These meetings helped to build a medium-term strategy based on a consensus among directors and cooperation among departments. Thus, company performance recovered rapidly.

Periodically the directors gather for a retreat (Figure 5-1). There have been 25 retreats since 1979, and the tradition has become an indispensable form for strategic discussions about the company. The management strategy for 1985 to 1990 is based on the results of a medium-term strategy deployed in the early half of the

1980s. It consists of sales, development, and product strategies (Figure 5-2). The long-term plan shown on the right side of the figure is the link by which the strategy is related to policy deployment.

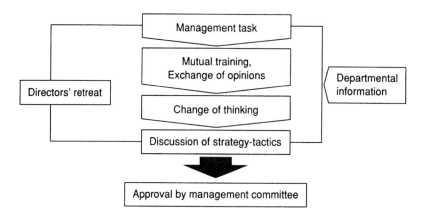

Figure 5-1. Role of Directors' Retreat (Aisin-Takaoka)

Types of Policy and Definitions

The management policy at this company calls for companywide priority actions as well as basic management. Figure 5-2 shows this system, including the management strategy.

Management Philosophy

The management philosophy, as already mentioned, is "creating a future with quality as supreme." This philosophy was established when TQC was introduced in order to implement quality management.

Management Vision

The management vision comprises the expected and targeted management strategy and long-term management planning.

Long-term Management Plan

The direction of management and priority tasks as a guideline for the next five years is a criteria for annual company policy. It is coded as "00T," the "00" corresponding to the last two digits of the calendar year. This year the company is looking at 90T planning.

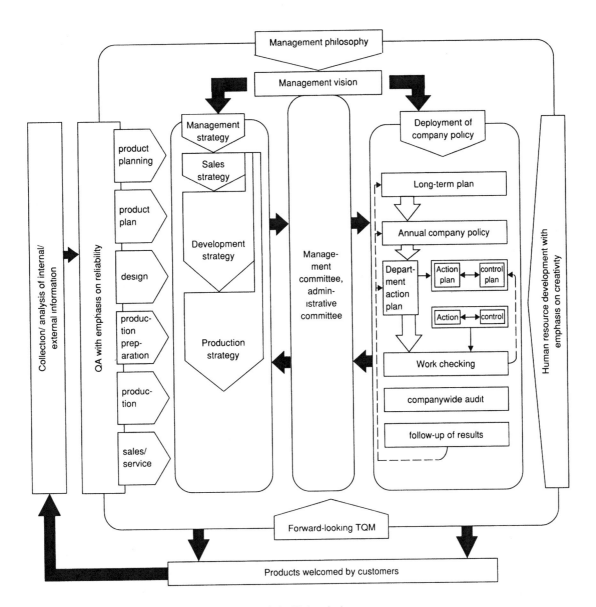

Figure 5-2. *Hoshin Kanri* **System Chart (Aisin-Takaoka)**

Annual Company Policy

The annual company policy is based on the long-term plan and the annual profit plan and priority tasks. It is deployed to department work action plans that are implemented by the department head that correspond to department policy.

Features of Annual *Hoshin Kanri*

At Aisin-Takaoka, the most important policy is shown in the long-term management plan, but responsibility for actual strategy implementation goes to annual company policy. It is important to perform a control cycle on the annual company policy.

In TQM, cross-functional (horizontal) deployment of a policy is favored over departmental (vertical) deployment. Deployment of policy in departments or offices is easy, but critical tasks that should be addressed interdepartmentally and tasks that have interdepartmental problems are often neglected. This company has introduced a system of linking the "department in charge" and "department taking action" (Figure 5-3). Cross-functional meetings are held, with the director in charge serving as chairperson of departmental deployment. The management function is classified into eight items (Figure 5-4), each function corresponding to a company policy classification.

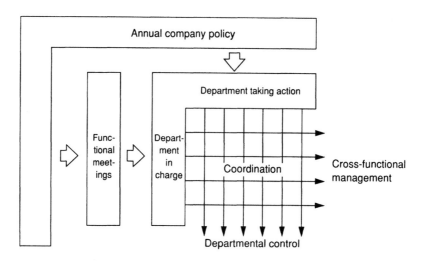

Figure 5-3. Deployment and Control of Company Policy

Department in Charge

Each target and means reflecting annual company policy items is assigned to a particular department in charge of its deployment. The department in charge establishes target-means values and supervises action undertaken by the action department. The department in charge also serves as an office for the cross-functional meeting.

Company Policy Classification	Cross-functional Management Meeting	Person in Charge	Department in Charge
Administration	Administrative meeting	○ ○ office	Business planning office
Sales	Sales meeting	△ △ office	Sales department
Research and development	R & D committee meeting	○ △ director	Development and planning office
Production	Production meeting	△ ○ office	Production
Quality	Quality meeting		
Cost	Cost meeting		
Human resources	Personnel training		
Health, safety and environment	Safety		

Figure 5-4. Company Policy Classification and Cross-functional Management Meeting

Action Department

Means are acted on in the daily work under the control of the department in charge. Deployment groups are not separated organizationally but are an action department within one's own department. The action department reports to the department in charge for supervision of the means deployment on the daily work level and for cross-functional meetings.

Structure of the Annual Company Policy

The annual company policy included six sections as shown in Figure 5-5 and briefly described below.

Annual theme. The annual theme focuses the purpose of the coming year and its challenges. It includes:

1. A brief outline of the company policy intentions for the year
2. The annual challenge to involve everyone

Slogan. These must be simple and easy to understand if everyone is to participate in implementing the annual policy. Some examples are listed:

1. Answer with quality
2. Shape the idea into a product
3. Eliminate waste

Management philosophy. This is the upper management's opportunity to clarify the vision in the context of TQM and the long-term strategy of the company — how the vision is to be achieved.

Intention. This makes the philosophy specific. It includes:

1. Analysis of last year's performance
2. Surrounding environment
3. Emphasis for this year

Annual policy. Assign priorities to tasks so as to reflect top management's policy. These tasks are the guidelines for the annual means. They are shown for each division of the company policy.

Annual target. The annual targets are expressed as specific expectations of the annual policy deployment action and can be controlled numerically.

Annual means. Listed are three to five means for each company policy division and the major tasks for achieving the annual policy and target. Annual means are taken up by the department work action plan of the department in charge of deployment.

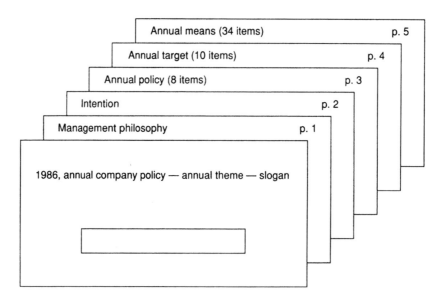

Figure 5-5. Structure of Annual Company Policy

Planning the Annual Company Policy

The company policy is established on January 1 of every year, but the fiscal year runs from March through the following February. The department section policy, which is based on the annual company policy, is planned during the two months before the start of the fiscal year and then acted on starting in March.

Thus, the annual company policy comprises projections about next year's environment, the long-term plan, instructions from top management, analysis of this year's policy deployment based on a companywide audit, and task priorities. Major tasks in the 1986 plan were to follow up on the commentary report of the Japan Quality Control Prize, as well as aiming for the PM award. An outline of the plan is shown in Figure 5-6.

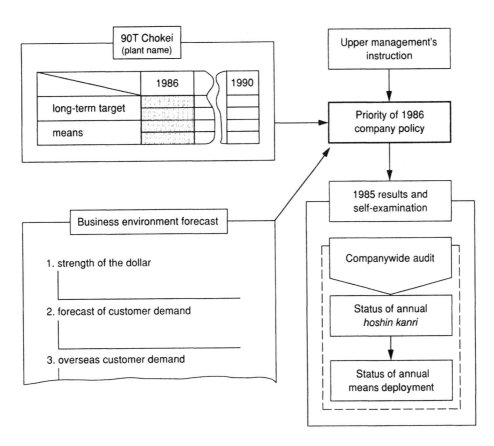

Figure 5-6. Background of 1986 Company Policy Planning

Steps in Planning Annual Company Policy

The status of the policy deployment for the current year is analyzed, its results reflected in next year's policy (see Figure 5-7). The director in charge fills in the coming year's company policy plan — that is, policy plan form 1 (Figure 5-8). This is based on a companywide audit, annual policy, target, means, and self-inspection. The management plan office, which is the office for companywide policy deployment, prepares a draft of the annual means based on the annual policy plan from each director. Next year's priority means are based on inspection of this year's results (Figure 5-9). These are shown to all the departments, and the judgment data for company policy means are summarized (Figure 5-10). The directors in charge and the departments submit input, which is coordinated with the policy means plan for review and planning of annual target items. The management plan office collects these annual policy target-means plans and submits them to the administrative committee for discussion.

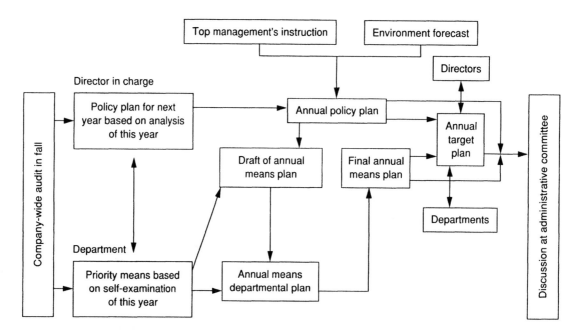

Figure 5-7. Steps in Planning Annual Company Policy

Departmental Deployment of the Annual Company Policy

The policy published at the beginning of the year is deployed into action plans for each department or section following the steps in Figure 5-11. These are

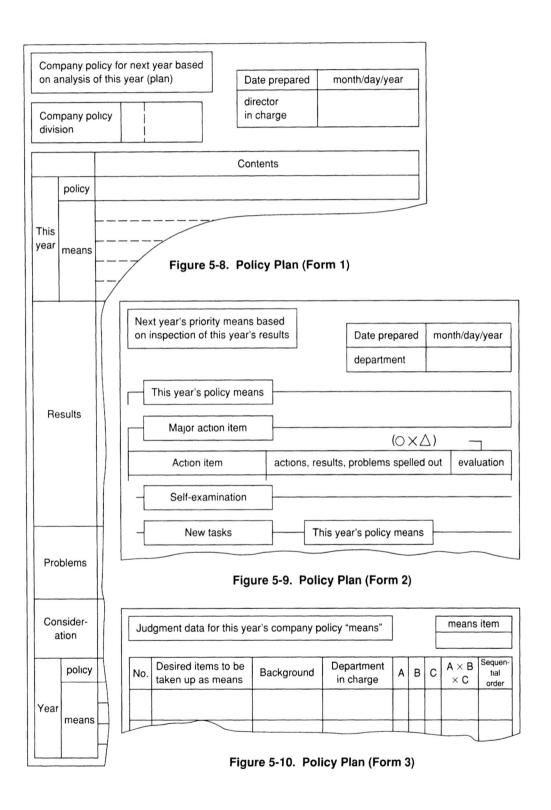

Figure 5-8. Policy Plan (Form 1)

Figure 5-9. Policy Plan (Form 2)

Figure 5-10. Policy Plan (Form 3)

used for taking actions after interfacing with daily activities. Heads of each department in charge prepare a major action item list for deployment of the annual company policy, as well as an action plan and target, which are discussed with the heads of the departments that will take action. They prepare a work action sheet for the department; this is used as department policy using form A (Figure 5-12). At this stage, the heads of the action departments determine which request items they want from the department in charge and select an action item based on discussion with the section heads of their own department. They then prepare a work action plan sheet for the department, using the same form (A). The department head draws up a work action plan sheet and shows it to the section heads, who then study major measures in coordination with the action department. The department in charge prepares a control plan sheet (Figure 5-11, form B1) and an annual target control sheet (Figure 5-11, form B2). On the basis of those sheets, the section head of the action department prepares a section plan as well as a work action plan sheet, using form C.

The department work action plan sheets are submitted to the management planning office and, after companywide adjustments and administrative committee approvals are implemented at the start of the year. The annual target is deployed into more specific control items and target values through this process.

Check/Follow-up

The deployment of the annual company policy is checked and followed up every month through the work-check and cross-functional meeting held by the director in charge and the department head. If anomalies occur, action is taken immediately. For example, each month the administrative committee checks on progress toward the annual target. The committee uses the company achievement status sheet, which evaluates the efforts of the departments at five stages, and the annual target check results report, which analyzes the achievement status of each department in charge. Furthermore, the progress of the policy deployment is checked, with an emphasis placed on departmental cooperation and the companywide audit, the latter performed every six months for the purpose of checking horizontal activities.

Companywide Audit

Twice a year the president audits the status of policy deployment in all departments and plants. The plan and its implementation are checked in the spring and fall, respectively. The companywide audit has the functions of (1) training the department and section heads in making presentations and (2) enhancing

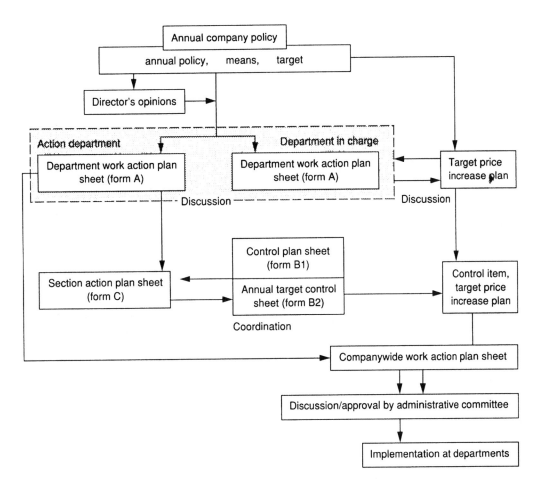

Figure 5-11. Deployment of Annual Company Policy

communication between the directors and employees. This is in addition to its original purpose of serving as the core of the company's TQC.

Supporting Information System for Policy Deployment

An important feature of Aisin-Takaoka's management control system is CAST, the company's computerized management information system. This consists of CAST-101, a financial simulation program that supports the long-term plan, and CAST-102, which assesses the health of the management on the basis of actual data. CAST-102 displays major management control items on a computer screen in graph form; at the same time, it offers additional functions of calculations, statistical measurements, and time sequential data analysis of the base data. This gives fast, multifaceted analyses. The status of progress toward the annual target can be confirmed on the graph screen.

Director	Department head

Page number	Department
	Office

Form A

Year, work plan sheet

Policy item	How to take up	Relation to others			Department action item	Section action item	Action department	
		When "a"	When "c"		No.	No.		Approval stamp
		policy code	department in charge	department/ section no.				

Section head in charge of own department	Target		Progress plan											What is abnormal? (control level)	Control data	Check frequency
	item	value	start								completion					
			3	4	5	6	7	8	9	10	11	12	1	2			

Figure 5-12. Work Action Plan Sheet

At present, we at Aisin-Takaoka are finding that tasks relating to new problems are having a greater impact on management than tasks relating to current problems. Much work in this area remains to be done, but we are confident that we can reach our target. We wish to learn from our implementation of TQC and to systematically deploy a comprehensive policy deployment system.

CASE STUDY 2: *HOSHIN KANRI* AT TOPPAN PRINTING

Toppan Printing Company is like many other companies that adopted policy deployment without thorough preparation. Normally, it takes about one to one and a half years of preparation to introduce policy deployment.

We assigned four hours of TQC education to the department and section heads for policy deployment, but understanding of *hoshin kanri* remained insufficient. A series of seminars held later took up the concept, resulting in deeper understanding of control items based on data. Presentations at these seminars of actual themes reinforced the importance of PDCA.

In addition, the TQC office created a policy deployment manual, which was well received.

TQC as a Means to Improve Company Structure

The company philosophy that "quality is supreme" translates into the actions of seeking out and solving problems in one's own department and one's own job, emphasizing process rather than results, orienting oneself to customer needs, and participating in a joint effort to achieve company goals. TQC is not a quick fix; rather, it is a proven means to strengthen the company structure.

Policy Deployment and Structural Improvement

Policy deployment is a tool for disseminating and implementing the president's policy in the face of change within and outside the organization. Policy deployment primarily consists of PDCA.

Terms Used in Policy Deployment

Key terms are *policy, target, means, control item, policy deployment, policy coordination, target deployment, plan, management plan,* and *daily control.*

To establish priorities, begin with an analysis of the previous year's performance. Focus on maintaining good results and improving poor results. Throughout the process, communicate with supervisors.

Control items are the yardstick of target achievement. Evaluating both results and means improves the morale of the people involved. After the TQC office distributed the policy deployment manual to all section heads, they asked them to prepare a priority measure action plan. The section heads then presented the plan at improvement seminars.

Assessment by the president or division head is important to the success of policy deployment. At Toppan Printing, the president prepared an assessment after one and a half years of TQC. Preparation for this assessment clarifies the department and section head policy and defines the specific action items and control items. As these assessments are repeated, an interdepartmental cooperation system can develop, helping to forge a broader range of organization under divisional policy.

The current policy is to improve customer satisfaction through QA. Customer satisfaction is attainable only as a sum of quality, delivery, cost, and seɪ ..ce, with the emphasis on quality. QA that requires horizontal (interdepartmental) control should be based on thorough daily control and *hoshin kanri*. After three years of TQC at this company, we are about to introduce cross-functional management. For this reason, enhanced *hoshin kanri* is both necessary and possible.

CASE STUDY 3: *HOSHIN KANRI* AT HOKURIKU KOGYO

Hokuriku Kogyo forges parts for equipment used in construction, agriculture, automobile manufacture, and other industries. We are an independent company with 130 employees and have our own system of planning, design, production, and sales. We introduced TQC in 1976 and received the Deming Prize in 1984. Our *hoshin kanri* is based on the concept of "clarifying things to be done by all departments and all employees" while emphasizing the process of the action. At the core of our system are *total attack forging* (TAF) activities.

The president began to relay his policy to workers around 1970 by informing them of his dreams and management targets. But specific means to realize them remained undefined, and deployment was insufficient. Instructions to department and section heads were well implemented, but there was no voluntary problem solving.

TQC was introduced in order to forge better control systems for the building of human resources. When TQC was introduced, the top managers attended a QC seminar; this was followed by QC study meetings with the department and section heads. First, workers studied the problems of the company. Next, they studied means for solving problems and achieving targets. Each department established action items, on which basis a companywide action plan list was prepared. It took about one year to come up with this prototype for a *hoshin kanri* system. Control and implementation of the annual policy was an important theme for the TQC committee. Unfortunately, deployment to the departments remained incomplete. Beginning in 1979, the president began to explain his annual policy to managers, after which he held a policy presentation meeting attended by all employees. The president's assessment was begun in 1983, at the same time that the department and section heads began to emphasize PDCA.

Thereafter, an annual policy was no longer sufficient; longer-term visions for the company management became necessary. As long-term management plans were made, top managers and department and section heads discussed long-term improvement plans and their means. Then they began preparing long-term priority action plans.

This process involved all employees and was named total attack forging (TAF). Since 1983 we have reviewed TAF annually, adding new tasks as necessary. The president's policy in May of every year takes into account results of a TAF activity, analysis of the previous year's results, and new external changes. The TQC committee deploys this policy into action items for each function. Thereafter, each department prepares a departmental action plan and a list of the control items.

A control graph is used for daily control. We analyze anomalies according to the handling rules and report them to supervisors on a defect corrective action form.

Every month the department head presents a monthly report to the cross-functional committee. Every six months the TQC office summarizes activities and evaluates target, means, and achievements on a structure evaluation sheet. Problems are then clarified for the next term plan.

Hokuriku Kogyo is small, so communication among top management and department and section heads occurs through daily activities. The president's assessment focuses on the PDCA cycle in each department and is intended to increase knowledge among top managers and heads of departments and sections. Each May and December departments and sections compile QC stories, reports, and other data for the president's assessment. The president's assessment report then targets items needing improvement, and these items become the basis of next term's improvement activities.

Since introducing policy deployment in 1976, we have found the process of implementing it to be one of trial and error. Specifically, we have learned the following:

- At the beginning, too much material was given to the department and section heads. Now they receive only necessary items; the rest are covered administratively.
- Improving control levels requires human resources.
- Targets must be backed up with means.
- Problems must be made visible, both within the department and within the company.

Because of our small size, we did our work as much as possible in our own way, without any particular glamour or wisdom. We know there is still much to be done.

CASE STUDY 4: *HOSHIN KANRI* AT KOBAYASHI KOSEI

Founded in 1946, Kobayashi Kosei is primarily a cosmetics manufacturer. The production center for this company introduced TQC in 1977, along with policy deployment. Since that time, the production center has become a pillar of control in the company.

The current system of policy deployment is the result of many improvements on the original system. Basic problems at the initial stage included the following:

1. Target and means deployment for the division head's policy were complex, and the means for action stages were unclear.
2. The relationship of means to target was not clearly understood.
3. The QC plan, cross-functional management, and policy deployment were separate from each other.
4. Duplications and omissions occurred from the deployment stage to the action plan.

Because these elements were important in the construction of our system, we eliminated the weaknesses. Our intention was to create a system in which

- A thorough analysis of last year's performance served as a base
- A matrix deployment of the target and means served as a base
- We could make systematic progress in the deployment of the target and means
- Deployment of the division head's priority plan could serve as the base for functional policy deployment

Structure of Policy Deployment

Policy deploymentat the production center is based on three policies:

1. Basic management
2. Medium-term management policy
3. Annual management policy

Figure 2-4 (Chapter 2) outlines the policy deployment program for this production center.

Planning the Annual Policy

The production center's annual policy comprises the policies of the production center (division) head, the department head, and the plant head; these policies are deployed in terms of targets and means. The emphasis is on a controllable system that clearly defines the relationship between a target and its causal factors.

The key here is analyzing last year's performance. Therefore, we arranged to emphasize that the results of last year's policy are thoroughly analyzed and summarized (Figure 2-6). This work is done at each organizational level and the results are incorporated into policy planning.

Target and causal factors and cause-effect relationships between these and the means (action items) are best arranged in the planning stage, and they must be used in the actual evaluation of performance.

Relation to QC Plan

The production center policy is planned on the basis of the division head's policy and a functional self-inspection of last year's results. In the past, the relationship between the QC plan and the policy has tended to be difficult to understand. Attention to the following points has clarified this relationship.

1. The means for implementing the division head's priorities through cross-functional management are classified into three groups:
   - Production center QA activities (led by the QA leader or QA committee)
   - Education, QC circle activities (led by TQC promotion committee)
   - Volume, cost activities (led by NPD committee or new production development)
2. A plan is made in which daily functional activities — for example, QA, education, QC circles, and safety — are added to the above means.

The above plan is published at the same time the production center policy is planned and has been positioned as an upper-level policy for the plant manager's policy planning.

Deployment of the Annual Policy

Relation of Target to Means

When planning of the upper policy begins, lower-level deployment activities are coordinated. Targets and means are deployed in the policies of each organizational level; that is, priority targets and means in upper-level policy are components of lower-level policy. Meanwhile, priority measures are added to the QC plan for means deployment at all levels.

Target-Means Relation Chart

A matrix chart clarifies the mutual cause-and-effect relationships between target and means deployments, to enhance compatibility among the section head, division head, and plant manager.

The relation of the target to means can be readily understood if last year's performance has been thoroughly analyzed (Figure 3-10).

Preparation of the Action Plan

On the basis of the target-means matrix, actual work begins with the preparation of an action plan sheet, on which a Gantt chart, an action in charge, and control items have been added to the action items. Figure 5-13 shows a policy relation matrix at the plant head level (Gumma plant).

Control Items for Policy Deployment

Control items are divided into control points and checkpoints at the production center. Figure 5-14 further classifies control items by application purposes.

The control items for policy deployment are divided into those that control the progress toward the target (deployed by arranging policy deployment) and those that control the means for implementation of the target.

The setup of control items for matrix deployment is indispensable in evaluating policy fulfillment. Control items are streamlined in the "control network" so that the relationship between control and policy for each job category is clear. Then they are made into a list. Control items for the policy are registered annually. Figure 5-15 shows how this is arranged.

Evaluation of Policy Fulfillment

Monthly Performance Reports

Control graphs that chart monthly performances are used here; the person in charge of control handles anomalies by analyzing variance.

Upper job classifications control their own control items. At the same time, they handle the anomalies in conjunction with control items if such anomalies continue to be in the control status of the subordinates.

Evaluation Method and Audit

One feature of policy deployment at Kobayashi Kosei is the objective, or numerical, evaluation. We use a target-means matrix chart to evaluate the status of targets and means in relation to the results and processes. The achievement rate and activity rate are evaluated in five levels according to the evaluation criteria of a two-element chart (Table 5-1). To measure the contribution of the means to the target, we use a coefficient (Table 5-2).

An evaluation target is set for each item in the policy relation matrix (Figure 5-13).

Evaluation target = [sigma] [(full score of 10 points) × (coefficient)]

The performance sum is the number of performance evaluation points accrued by a control item during a certain period (Table 5-3). The achievement rate equals the ratio of performance evaluation points to target evaluation points (Table 5-4).

A policy audit is performed, based on the departmental audit, division audit, and top level corporate audit, where PDCA occurs.

One example of a complete cycle deployed from Figure 5-13 is shown below in Figure 5-16.

19-- Gumma plant, plant head's policy	Classification		
Departmental action target and department/section action items, matrix	Function no.		
	Functional classification		

Plant head	QC section head

Func-tional classi-fication	Priority action item	No.	Action item	Actual — Cost — productivity index (C 1 R)	automation line operating rate (1 1 R)	product inventory /month (1 2 R)	new item inventory /month (1 1 R)	new product major claim (Q 2 R)	Target — QA 1 — shipment claim, versus last year (II 4 R)	Education 4 — QC circle with >3 theme completion (IV 5 R)	no. of improvement suggestions per QC circle (IV 6 R)	Safety 5 — off-work accident (IV 7 R)	Registra-tion no.	Control item	Control data
Gumma plant	Arrange works under new work system and build in production plan that enables effective use of production elements	1.1	Close relation with upstream for production of new product on automated line	◎	◎	○	○							No. of new product automation	
		1.2	Assure transfer of product to utilize functions and features of Gumma plant	◎	○										
		1.3	Review bulk production process pattern for more production	○	◎	○								Raw material inventory $ amount	
			Active participation in engineering project	○	◎									W/H change	
Cost	progress in rationalization by increased review of indirect offices			◎	◎	◎								Indirect labor	
		5.1	Enhance relation to development department for improved DR contents and ——											DR implemen-tation rate	

		Control items →	productivity index	rate of utilization of automated line	product inventory	new item, 000 inventory per month	new product major claims	no. of shipment claims	no. of QC circles completing more than 3 themes	no of improvement proposals	no. of work accidents	Rate of prevention of quality trouble	Outsource evaluation	No. of claim of automation	Rate of participation in seminars	No. of theme completions/ proposals	No. of off-work accidents
QA	5.2	Enhance building-in of quality at mass production preparation stage; assure quality of new product / Enhanced stability test and prevention of trouble through proper action					◎					″					
	5.3	Guidance of outsources for maintenance/ improvement of material quality					◎						″				
		Establish process control for automation		○			◎							″			
		Guide transportation contractors for reduction in claims					◎								″		
	8.1	Reduce time of mass production preparation stage / Enhance one-side evaluation capability of prescription for shorter delivery time		○			○	◎	◎							″	
Safety		Promotion of safety control									◎						″
		Control item registration no.	C 1 R · 9	I 1 R · 2	I 2 R 9		Q 2 R · 9	II 4 R · 7	IV 5 R · 9	IV 6 R · 4	IV 7 R · 7						
		Control data	control graph	control graph	control graph	control graph	control graph	control graph	control graph	control graph	control graph						

(1) Control item corresponding to target is assigned control item no. corresponding to means and is coded to person in charge

(2) Control item corresponding to means is assigned control item no. corresponding to target and is coded to person in charge.

(3) Control items for target are the control points on matrix of each involved individual, and control items for means are mainly checkpoints to check processes.

Figure 5-13. Policy Relation Matrix (Gumma Plant)

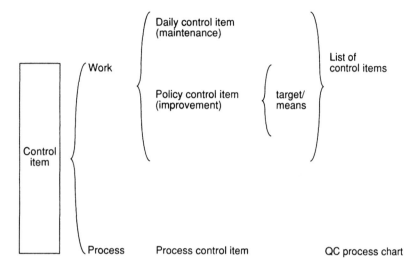

Figure 5-14. Classification of Control Items by Purpose

Job study form

(job title) Gumma plant manager	(person in charge) Plant manager	Job content × × × × × ×	
Present job (by function)	Information/data for judgment	Judgment criteria	Handling method

Control items of policy

19—, Gumma plant head policy

Matrix, departmental action target and department/section head items

	plant head	QC section head
Gumma plant		

Classification		Target			Control item:	Control data
Function no.						
Functional classification	QA		Educa-tion			
Number						
Action target		ship-ping claims com-pared to last year	QC circles com-pleting more than 3 themes			

Func-tional classi-fication	Priority action item	No.	Action items	new product: major claims			Control item:	Control data
Element	Arrange work under new system for effective use of production element		Close relation with upstream for production of new product on automated line				No. of new product automation	control graph
			Assure transfer of product to utilize functions and features of Gumma plant				Amount of new product production	"
QA	Enhance building in of quality at mass production preparation stage		Enhance relation to develop-ment department for im-proved DR contents & ----	◎			DR imple-mentation	"
			Enhanced stability test and prevention of trouble through proper action	◎			Rate of pre-venting quality problems	"
			Guidance of outsources for maintenance/improvement of material quality	◎			Outsource evaluation	"
Control item registration no.						no. of QC circles com-pleting more than 3 themes		
Control items				new product: major claims	no of ship-ment claims			
Control data				control graph	control graph	control graph		

Figure 5-15. Control Items (Gumma Plant)

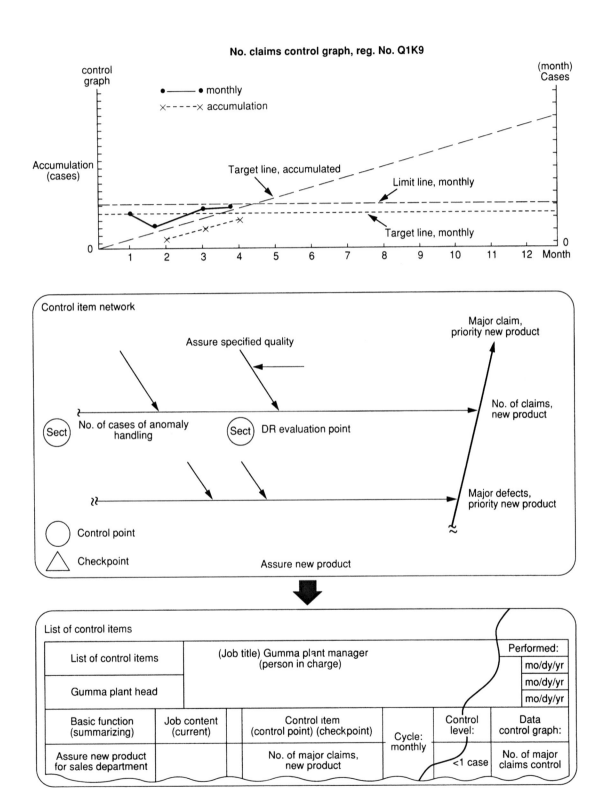

No. claims control graph, reg. No. Q1K9

control graph

●——● monthly
×----× accumulation

Accumulation (cases)

Target line, accumulated

Limit line, monthly

Target line, monthly

(month) Cases

0

1 2 3 4 5 6 7 8 9 10 11 12 Month

Control item network

Assure specified quality

Major claim, priority new product

(Sect) No. of cases of anomaly handling

(Sect) DR evaluation point

No. of claims, new product

Major defects, priority new product

◯ Control point

△ Checkpoint

Assure new product

List of control items

List of control items	(Job title) Gumma plant manager (person in charge)		Performed:	
			mo/dy/yr	
Gumma plant head			mo/dy/yr	
			mo/dy/yr	
Basic function (summarizing)	Job content (current)	Control item (control point) (checkpoint)	Cycle: monthly	Control level:	Data control graph:
Assure new product for sales department		No. of major claims, new product		<1 case	No. of major claims control

Table 5-1. Evaluation Criteria

			Rate of target achievement				
			←Good			Bad→	
		5-level evaluation	5	4	3	2	1
Rate of means imple- mentation	Good ↑	5	10	9	8	7	6
		4	9	8	7	6	5
		3	8	7	6	5	4
	Bad ↓	2	7	6	5	4	3
		1	6	5	4	3	2

Table 5-2. Degree of Correspondence, Coefficients

Code for correspondence	Degree of correspondence	Coefficient
	Very strong	100%
	Strong	50%
No mark	None	0%

Table 5-3. Calculation of Evaluation Target Point

Means \ Target	Target 1	Target 2	Target 3	Evaluation target point
Means 1	10	10	5	25 points
Means 2	5	10	10	15
Means 3	5			15
Evaluation target point	20 points	20	15	55 / 55

(10 pt. × 0.5)
↑
correspondence coefficient

Full score, 10 points

Correspondence coefficient
↓
(8 pt. × 0.5)
↑
From evaluation criteria table

Table 5-4. *Hoshin Kanri* Evaluation

Means \ Target / 5-level evaluation		Target 1 — 5	Target 2 — 4	Target 3 — 2	Performance evaluation points	Evaluation target points	Means implementation rate
Means 1	5	10	9	3.5	22.5	25	90.0%
Means 2	3	4		5	9.0	15	60.0%
Means 3	3	4	7		11.0	15	73.3%
Performance evaluation points		18.0	16.0	8.5	42.5 / 42.5	55	✕
Evaluation target points		20	20	15	55	Overall achievement rate	
Target achievement rate		90.0%	80.0%	56.7%	✕	$\dfrac{42.5}{55} = 77.3\%$	

Step 1

Step 2, 19--, Product center head's policy

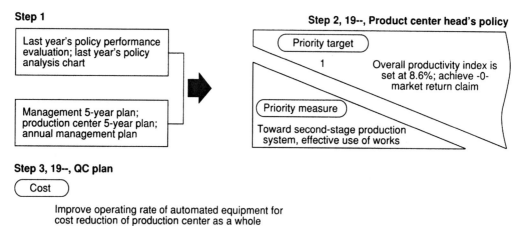

Step 3, 19--, QC plan

(Cost)

Improve operating rate of automated equipment for
cost reduction of production center as a whole

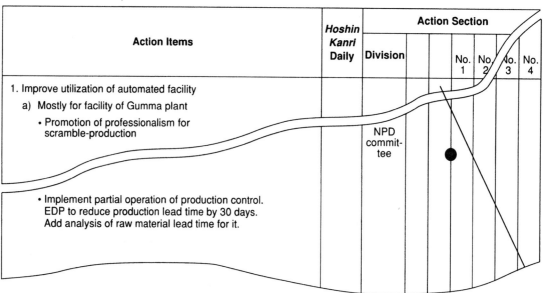

Figure 5-16. Complete Deployment Cycle

Step 4, -- Plant, target deployment chart

    Target deployment chart

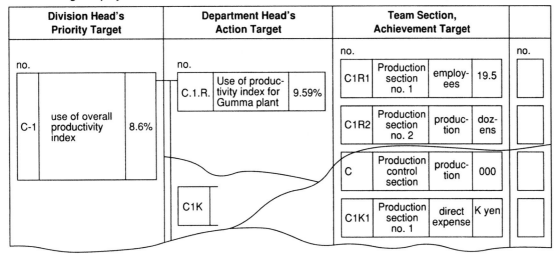

Division Head's Priority Target			Department Head's Action Target			Team Section, Achievement Target				
no.			no.			no.				no.
C-1	use of overall productivity index	8.6%	C.1.R.	Use of productivity index for Gumma plant	9.59%	C1R1	Production section no. 1	employees	19.5	
						C1R2	Production section no. 2	production	dozens	
						C	Production control section	production	000	
			C1K			C1K1	Production section no. 1	direct expense	K yen	

Step 5 – Plant, priority measures deployment chart

    Chart 1 (division head - department head - section head)

Division Head's Policy Priority Measures	Relation Lines	Department Head's Policy Priority Action Item	Relation Lines	Section Action Items	Action Section
1. Buildup of second production system for better rationalization (1) Effective use of shifts (2) Start building second production system with this year as origin point	●—▶●	1.1 Effective use of product element by arranging works under new work system, 1.1.1 Closer tie with upstream for new product production in automated line	●—▶● ●◀— ●◀—	1.1.5 Closer tie with externals-design stages for smooth production of new products	QC section (Gumma plant) Prod. no. 1 (") Prod. no. 1 (")

> Items department head implements among action items deployed from priority action items

1) Priority action items are deployed to action items; some items are not delegated to section head but are implemented by department head

Step 6. Target-means matrix

Step 7. Determination on control items

Step 8. Implementation, evaluation, handling

CHAPTER 6

Hoshin Kanri as a Part of TQM: A Roundtable Discussion

Introductory Remarks

Nomi: As a start, I would like to ask Professor Akao, as an experienced leader in the field, what are the fundamental issues of policy deployment.

Fundamental Issues

Akao: In recent years companies have tended to approach policy deployment from the standpoint of countermeasures alone, failing to fully analyze their own situations. They proceed on the basis of a Gantt chart on which they have simply listed measures to be taken for the next year to satisfy incompletely thought out goals.

What we have done in quality control is to first set our themes and then collect data in accordance with those themes. Next, we analyze the data in various ways to determine how they relate to underlying causal factors; on that basis, we draw a diagram of specific causes. We are then in a position to identify the barriers to, for example, lowering the rate of defects or overcoming stagnation. Only then are we able to formulate measures to be taken.

This is the process by which quality control became established in Japan. However, companies often bypass the collection and analysis of data and go directly to formulating countermeasures. In policy deployment as a part of TQM, it is essential to fully analyze the causal factors before formulating any measures. For example, we should review the various things we did the past year and identify the problems we faced. That means drawing up a cause-and-effect diagram, examining it thoroughly to identify bottlenecks (which are problems of process), and then formulating means to remove those bottlenecks.

This does not mean, however, that all appropriate means can be formulated at once. They should be tried and results checked on a monthly basis and shown on a control chart. And, if the results are inadequate, you need to return to the cause-and-effect diagram for a thorough reexamination and add whatever countermeasures seem lacking. Repetition of this PDCA process on a monthly basis is essential to implementing policy deployment as part of TQM.

Nomi: I remember your saying that in policy deployment it is important not only to look at outcomes but also to analyze the process carefully and solve the problems of quality control. I thank you, Professor Akao, for pointing out the problem of taking a too-formalistic or all-encompassing approach to policy deployment. Now I would like to ask Mr. Koura to share with us his current thoughts on policy deployment.

Koura: Clearly, there is confusion about the system, which has been introduced only recently. First, there is the problem of targets. In the development of means, we usually start with a list of important actions to be taken, such as those of the section chiefs based on policies set by the department head. Next, ordinarily, targets would be set, values assigned, and time schedules worked out for the pursuit of such targets. But there is often a blank at this point. Sometimes, values are entered where targets should be. Even worse, some people write down target-values where they should enter targets. In other words, they enter the control objectives but set no quantitative value for the targets. Thus, the specific targets remain unclear.

Second, there is a tendency to merely list things — that is, to simply list means. No priorities are set. Even though I keep insisting that provisions be made for feedback in the following year, people (especially beginners with little understanding) fail to incorporate CA (check-act), as Professor Akao mentioned, and immediately list the means.

The list of means, if it evolves from intermediate plans, tends to consist of actions that are undertaken on more or less a daily basis and are easily drawn from experience or one's job situation. You can thus end up with a long list of means but have no sense of which means take priority for the coming year.

Akao: In this context, some people set up the means and then assign a goal-value to each mean, one by one. Actually, this is the opposite of what should be done. The implementation of means can be checked on a Gantt chart. Targets, or aims, should be set before means are formulated. The latter should occur only after the current level of achievement in relation to the targets is determined and the reasons for any shortfall are identified. Thus, the means evolve from the targets. Yet many plans of action fail to include basic targets; they have only means that they then assign targets. Therefore, many are managing by setting as targets what in fact are means. This is not a good idea.

Koura: People essentially are poor at gathering data. They don't understand what constitutes data.

Akao: In my case, I do not have people go directly into policy deployment without studying quality control. For the first six months to a year, they study quality control by focusing on themes set by departments and sections; they must come up with solutions by going through the PDCA cycle. They are then gradually introduced to policy deployment as the problems of each department are clearly identified. When policy deployment is introduced outside the context of quality control, it is certain to become formalistic. Studying quality control is a fundamental prerequisite to the introduction of policy deployment.

Koura: There is another thing, which can be illustrated by giving an example. When a certain company was setting targets, there was disagreement among the top managers (factory manager, branch office manager, and so on) and various department heads, so adjustments had to be made. The problem, it was decided, would be dealt with at a directors meeting. During the discussion, each factory or branch office would learn how much it was to achieve once the company's overall annual target was allocated.

To achieve its assigned target, each unit slightly overstated its targets. Thus, the factory manager would set his or her unit's goal above what the head office targeted for the unit and accept the responsibility of achieving it. The heads of departments, on the other hand, submitted their targets on the basis of what they thought they could realistically achieve. It would be unreasonable, in their view, to ask them to do more.

The top managers indicated that they would be satisfied to check the various conditions of target attainment within the context of policy deployment. But the departments asserted that such an approach was unacceptable since they could not possibly attain the target set by the branch, even with their best effort.

Eventually, all decided to consider the company target as a target for which each unit is responsible and the unit's larger target as something that could be achieved if all went well. The closing of the gap between the two targets was interpreted as being dependent on the leadership capacity of the branch managers. Thus, a strategy committee of the branch managers was inaugurated to deal with important projects, and the branch managers were given an opportunity to get involved in actual operations. For example, if methods of sales were involved, branch managers and the like could actively participate in making a big sale.

Such sales are not possible without knowing about the market. To achieve such a target the strategy committee must deal with the more important problems facing branch managers. In this way, the target that had to be achieved and the target that might be achieved were mutually agreed on. In short, it is possible to set a target of possibility and a target of planned operation. The difficulty arises in having to adjust the discrepancy between the two targets. This is a rather good example of how such a problem was resolved.

Akao: In connection with graphs used to chart progress, management by results is often used to good effect — that is, if the results are all right. Most typical of this approach is the flag system adopted by the Komatsu Manufacturing

Company. Under this system, the targets are formulated very rationally; unfortunately, only the results are emphasized.

To attain a goal, after all, is to bring the current level up to the targeted level. *Level* in this context refers to the level of the operational process that engenders the goal attributes. Since it is this level that we want to improve, we need to search for the causes underlying problems and then formulate means to deal with those causes.

Neither should means be formulated prematurely nor targets be set by themselves. We must have concrete means that specifically move us toward our targets. This means that we need a plan of action that skillfully integrates the targets and means, and we need to perform the PDCA cycle on a monthly basis.

Koura: What you have just said about checking the process in various ways involving not only targets but also means corresponds to the function of what I referred to as the strategy committee. There would be discussions at the committee's monthly meetings. Means introduced at the beginning of the year could develop in various ways, sometimes positively and other times negatively.

How to Determine Target Values and Means

Nomi: Essentially, this means there is a need to review the results attained in the preceding year. It is important to collect data on priority items, analyze the process using QC methods, identify the causal factors, and accordingly set in clear fashion the goal-values and the appropriate means. Since this is an important point, can you extend your discussion a step further?

Akao: To set annual policies correctly, companies must review the previous year's performance. This is so important that some companies prefer CAPD (check, act, plan, do) to the more usual PDCA. The appropriateness of targets and means set this year depends on how thoroughly the results of last year are reviewed.

What we commonly see is a company giving up on plans in November or December, celebrating the year's end, and drinking to renewed efforts in the new year. In January the company draws up a plan once more, but come December it is given up again. This is what Professor Ikezawa of Waseda University calls "plan-plan management."* We can conclude that the most important thing in policy deployment for TQM is that there is an analysis of the previous stage.

---

* The Japanese word "plan-plan" used here is a pun; it means both "only planning" and also "sloppy."

In addition, when the company undertakes strategic planning it is necessary to not only examine past problems but project future changes in the environment and articulate aims for the future.

Nomi: Do you have anything to add, Mr. Koura? For example, can we use the CA chart?

Koura: Once, when Mr. Akao and I jointly directed a policy deployment study group in the business operation division of a certain company, we suggested that a CA chart be drawn up first. However, we had to explain how to go about it three or four times before the group understood and finally produced one. Similar charts in various forms are available in many companies. At Kobayashi Kosei, for example, there is the *performance analysis chart*. Each company should prepare a chart that fits its situation, but in any case, the emphasis should be on CA. This company calls it simply the CA chart.

Nomi: There is a tendency in companies writing hoshin statements to simply list means without first conducting needed studies and analyses. They are concerned more with the appearance than with the content. It is more important to base listings of problems and analysis reports on a year-end review of results. Could we discuss this further, in more concrete terms?

Koura: I brought with me an actual chart. We are now talking about performance in the past, but when we set operational plans we anticipate the year-end results generally about three months in advance. At that time we identify the problem areas and set the policies of the different department heads. The procedures differ according to company, as we try to keep things more or less fluid rather than fixed. At about this stage, each department, taking into consideration the policies of top managers, plans its performance for the current year. It is here, in talking about the current year's performance, that the CA chart comes into play.

We have tentatively titled the chart the CA, or check-action, chart. If for the current year, the target of, say, annual sales is not met, a variety of problems related to the shortfall is listed. The listing would be an itemization of each reason reviewed in relation to the identified problems. In this way, a diagram of specific reasons is prepared for each problem.

For example, factors responsible for problem 1 would be selected by all. These factors might be identified as ABCDE. Now, the question is whether ABCDE indeed comprise negative elements, and a Pareto analysis is suggested as a way to determine this. If such an analysis is done to determine what percent is lost because of factor A and what percent because of factor B, then weights can be assigned to each factor. We can continue this analysis for each factor, and so the procedure becomes quite detailed.

Akao: To supplement a little, this procedure facilitates our formulation of means. It is surprisingly difficult to set objectives. We would first consider the effect that is expected and, if the policies of top management are made explicit, we would set our own management objectives in accordance with those policies. In other words, top management's policies become specific management objectives and thus, ipso facto, our specific targets.

Once we have our specific targets, we reverse the procedure and once again select our means. We have as a result a plan of action that incorporates our targets and the means needed for attaining them. The CA chart, in this way, is nothing more than a preparatory step to a plan of action. A plan of action based on means prematurely selected differs greatly from one developed in the way just described. Such a process is very important.

Nomi: So far you have pointed out the problems associated with ways to set up plans. Is it correct to conclude that CA is important for setting up plans rationally and that the CA chart is a means to facilitate that?

Akao: Yes, but since CA is done within a limited time, sometimes it is still not sufficient. You would check things on a control chart and, if things still aren't going well, you would reanalyze the situation. This is the most important point. A viable measure emerges, and that is added to the plan of action. This constitutes the monthly PDCA, which must be implemented for success. I don't think you can succeed by setting the annual targets and then simply going by the plan of action.

Nomi: Do you mean that it is necessary above all to check things regularly on a monthly basis?

Akao: The danger in stating it that way is that you might think that all you need to do is to check things only once a month. It should be understood that results obtained on a monthly basis are the results of all that take place during the preceding month. Ultimately, there is a relationship to daily management. Since it is the culmination of the total management effort, including daily management, management grounded in daily attention to causal factors is more important than simply examining results once a month.

Koura: Some companies seem to operate in this fashion. They distinguish between management items focused on results and those focused on causes.

Akao: I have been recommending such a distinction in recent years. People have told us they don't understand the meaning of the terms *control items* and *check items*. Therefore, I have tried to avoid using too many terms.

Koura: You have reduced the jargon to a single term, *control items*, and introduced a distinction between a focus on causal factors and a focus on results.

Akao: The point is, it is not enough to do something just once a month; you must have firm control over control items focused on causal factors on a weekly and daily basis.

Koura: It would be nice if such ideas spread through the use of terminology. The terms have become more sophisticated. At one time, the terms *control items* and *check items* were used, but I guess the newer terms are better.

Akao: They are all right as far as the meanings go, but these new terms are offered only to facilitate understanding, since the older terms tend to be misunderstood.

How to Determine the Control Items

Nomi: Since we are talking about control items, can you explain how to set them up, especially how to prevent them from becoming too formalistic?

Koura: That is difficult. The best thing is to apply a Pareto analysis of, say, the amount of sales or the rate of defects and let the resulting numerical values serve as the targets for each means. Things don't often work out ideally, however. By "control items," do we mean items that are used in the context of policy deployment to check against on the basis of results obtained at the end of a month or a year?

Akao: There are many different definitions, of course. Strictly speaking, we would plot on a graph the outcome of our action after, say, one month — focusing, in other words, on results. The quality of the results depends on what was done during the preceding month. In short, the results are tied to a process. Poor results are always due to problems in the process. And so, we do something about the process.

In terms of PDCA, this means first setting a *plan*, and then *doing*, *checking*, and taking *action*. We would draw a graph based on these activities and try to bring our performance up to a certain level by identifying bottlenecks and formulating means to remove them. If, in following the plan of action, we should run into difficulties, we would reanalyze the situation. If the problem rests with the original plan of action, we would revise that plan. What we are doing, in effect, is following the PDCA cycle.

Thus, the basic items needed to pursue the PDCA cycle would constitute the most important control items. These are what we call control items focused on results. For effective results, however, we would have to check on a weekly or daily basis several important causal factors among the many preceding the outcome. These would constitute the control items focused on causal factors. In the past, they were referred to as *check items*, but to facilitate understanding they are here called *control items focused on causal factors*.

On a control chart, a target line sloping upward (meaning "better outcome") would represent a control item for improvement, whereas one that is level would represent a control item for maintenance. For this reason, in the case of daily management, items for maintenance would be numerous. This would be particularly so when daily checks are involved. This is most typically represented in a control chart.

How to Effectively Use Control Items

Nomi: I am often told that people do not understand how control items are worked out between supervisors and subordinates or between the main office and the branches. I wonder if you could address this issue at the most basic level.

Akao: Whether one sees an item as focused on results or on causes is purely a matter of perspective. A supervisor may see an item in terms of causes, but if it is the result of his own efforts and an excellent one, he can claim it without hesitation as a control item for him. If, on the other hand, it is a causal factor for some other result, then from his perspective it can be defined as that kind of control item.

Koura: If we were to show the control items graphically in terms of specific causes, this means some of the control items identified for a department head may very well be those of a section chief. If these distinctions can be shown clearly in a graph, that would be the best way to understand all this. But this is a difficult thing to do. It is, however, a topic for future studies.

Akao: One other point: A typical mode of showing the linkages between targets is the flag system. This is the system conceived some 25 to 26 years ago by Nokawa Shoji, then president of the Komatsu Manufacturing Company. He developed the system while working out a set of control items for that company as it aimed to win the Deming Prize. This system combines the graph based on specific causes and one based on a Pareto analysis. Flags are lined up to represent targets, and the aim is to reduce the causal factors weighted according to the Pareto analysis.

This system is still the best method available today for working out the targets, but concerns about it remain. Sometimes it works well and sometimes it doesn't. One of the concerns involves the relationship between a supervisor and a subordinate, which was mentioned. Essentially, it makes little sense to view the display of flags in its entirety. What is important is to identify the group for which each flag represents a control item.

Thus, a supervisor would need be concerned only with his or her flags (targets) and not with those of his or her subordinates, although it would be necessary to keep informed about them. Knowing about them, however, is not the same as having to take action. And so, a control item that does not call for action cannot exist. I set as a condition for proprietorship of a control item the possibility of taking at least one action against the causal factors. Workers must therefore take responsibility for their own control items and at their own level implement the PDCA cycle. Otherwise, even the flag system will not work.

On the flag itself, an arrow points upward. This is important because, even though the flags represent specific causal factors, the fact that the arrows point upward indicates that the effort to attain the targets is concentrated in a upward vector. If this were control by norms, the arrows would point downward. Such an approach would invariably lead to failure. In fact, there are many examples of failure. I believe it is very important to mobilize everyone's effort upward.

Another requirement is for workers to take each flag as their own control item and implement the PDCA cycle at their particular level.

Koura: Mathematically and logically speaking, if each person would take the responsibility to meet his or her own targets, the targets of the top management would presumably be attained.

Akao: One more thing: If your targets are met but the subordinates' are not, you needn't do anything. The subordinates would have to take action for themselves. If, however, the failures of a few subordinates should affect your efforts, then you as the supervisor would have to take action. It is necessary to make these distinctions.

Koura: It would thus be wise to keep abreast of your subordinates' progress.

Akao: It is important to possess such information.

Koura: It would be nice if these matters could be evaluated and guidance offered through meetings.

Akao: It would be quite all right for supervisors to guide their subordinates on what actions they have taken or are about to take. The worst thing supervisors can do is check only the results and give out orders. They need, rather, to guide the subordinates on their actions based on their own control items and PDCA activities.

Koura: I wonder if the real meaning of checking doesn't lie somewhere in this discussion.

Relationship of *Hoshin Kanri* to Daily Management

Nomi: Thank you for discussing the many important points of policy deployment. Since the relationship between policy deployment and daily management emerges as a fresh issue, can you address this next?

Koura: In any company, policy deployment, addressing as it does important issues, makes a roughly 80 percent contribution to management in general. In terms of time allocated, however, the 80 percent contribution belongs to daily management. We tell our clients to keep this kind of perspective. We frequently remind them that policy deployment will suffer if it is not grounded in daily management.

There is a historical background to this relationship. When Nippon Kayaku Company leaders worked on their control items, they did so from the perspective of daily management. That is, they took the standpoint of the separate duties assigned to the operational units. Komatsu's management, on the other hand, developed their control items from the operational plans, or from the standpoint of attaining the annual targets. These two approaches are bound to make contact at some point. If examined on a summary chart, some control items could be distinguished as hoshin items or daily control items, while others would have elements common to both approaches. It is in the latter category that we would find concrete points of contact between the two.

Akao: The tendency in recent years has been to make these ideas complex, but I try to think of them in simple terms. What I mean is, even companies not using policy deployment practice daily management. Company operations are necessarily based on past practices, manuals, or standards. Each of these constitutes daily management.

When a company inquires into problems and areas needing modification, it is setting its targets and policies. Thus, policy deployment involves the handling of priority problems and the efforts to break away from the status quo. In short, the attempt to introduce changes in the current (daily) management system constitutes *hoshin kanri* or policy deployment. This means that with daily management as the base, important issues would be taken up and addressed as policy deployment.

Koura: We discussed how daily management and policy deployment work out in the context of departmental or functional management and cross-functional management. We looked at the relationship as one involving differential weights. In departmental or functional management, both are fully involved. In cross-functional management, the role of the cross-functional management committee is to plan and to diagnose. In functional management, both policy deployment and daily management are regarded as equally important and are both given double circles (for strong influence). In cross-functional management, policy deployment receives greater emphasis. It receives the double circle, while daily management receives a single circle. (See Table 2-8.)

Akao: In the context of guaranteeing quality in cross-functional management, there are, for example, summary tables of quality control activities or charts summarizing the quality assurance system. Operating on the basis of these would constitute daily management.

Relationship to Cross-functional Management

Nomi: In this connection, can you, Mr. Akao, describe the problems associated with cross-functional management? You have been pointing them out for some time now.

Akao: Even cross-functional management has as its base functional management. There are departments responsible for guaranteeing quality, managing profits, or managing quantity, for example. They have names like the department of quality assurance, the department of quality control, the department of cost management, and the department of production management. Cross-functional management occurs when these departments carry out their respective responsibilities with an eye toward other departments. In large companies, it is difficult for any one department to look at matters from this companywide standpoint. In Japan, it was to address this problem that cross-functional management evolved.

Since the English word *function* commonly refers to activities associated with a particular job or office, we use the term *cross-functional management*. But it is important not to ignore the distinction between the concepts of cross-functional management and the management of "job activities." To implement cross-functional management, you need to set up special committees to address, for example, quality assurance issues. Several companies, including Toyota and Komatsu, have done this successfully. But setting up formal structures is no guarantee of success.

For example, when a certain company with just a single factory tried to implement cross-functional management in various areas, the same faces would appear in every committee meeting. In this kind of situation, you would need to organize one steering committee and then separate the topics for discussion according to operational levels, or appoint subcommittees, for example.

Koura: It is important to think in terms of improving the overall system.

Akao: One type of failure involving a committee for cross-functional management is making excessive effort to address claims of quality defects. Such problems should be addressed in meetings called for those specific purposes. Especially when the purpose is for quality assurance, it should take up, as suggested by Mr. Koura, the underlying conditions. If, for example, claims are to be discussed, the aim should be to identify those faulty conditions that led to the claims. It is important to realize that the aim of action should be directed toward the underlying conditions and not toward the claims as such.

Nomi: Well put. The problem is not the claim itself but the faulty conditions that led to the claim. Any action taken should address those underlying conditions.

Koura: This means advancing efforts in quality control. Some people think it is better to introduce cross-functional management not as the antidote to a bad performance but as part of a multi-pronged attempt to improve the situation, through coordination of policy deployment with daily management. Thus, from the point of view of introducing TQM, you should attempt a variety of improvement activities and move toward policy deployment. Once things begin to work smoothly, extend your effort to daily management and perfect the structural arrangements.

All the problems are likely to be identified in this process. I believe that improvement of the overall system is best accomplished through a linking of problems together.

Nomi: The more formalistic the policy deployment system, the more it raises questions such as how many control items belong to daily management and how many to policy deployment, and how best to distinguish between the two. Given that daily management is at the base, however you approach policy deployment, it is essential to keep your feet on the ground, as all of you have been saying.

Akao: The focus should not be on forms. Rather, the effort should begin with identifying the important themes of the various problems, then gradually move toward policy deployment, and finally firmly organize efforts at daily management. Even with daily management, since there are many items to check, you should make sure that none of the important points are missed. You do this by using Pareto analyses. You needn't be overly concerned with details like numbers.

Even if you set targets through policy deployment, the ultimate object of action is the system itself, and so useful conclusions would necessarily be standardized. In this way, everything would be absorbed into daily management. This is what we mean by a management system or management levels. What is identified as faulty is taken up at the level of policy deployment, and the revised approaches are applied at the level of daily management. In the end, the base is daily management.

Nomi: I think these are the most important points. Even small companies try first to set up the forms when they introduce policy deployment as part of their TQM program. As Mr. Akao mentioned, even companies that have only one factory will, for the purpose of cross-functional management, form a special committee, as the larger companies do.

Koura: Every company seeks a model. While it is all right to seek a model, each company should, on examining the model, consider how to apply it to its own particular circumstances.

Akao: What is most frightening is when a company introducing policy deployment hands out a manual prepared by someone in the head office and attempts to implement the system before anyone understands it. This causes a lot of problems. One company, on the other hand, reversed this approach, dealing first with the most important problems. After that, it worked on policies at the branch manager's level. In the following year, it developed policies at the main office and finally got to the policies at the company president's level. This approach would seem to be, if anything, more natural.

QC for Strategic Management

Nomi: Mr. Koura, you wrote about product-based management in the August 1986 issue of *Standardization and Quality Control*, a special edition on cross-functional management and standardization. In recent years, we are seeing policy deployment rapidly developing and diversifying along lines such as the place of product-based management or the problem of strategic management, which Mr. Akao referred to earlier.

Akao: Mr. Mochimoto, the current president of Nichi Pura, has spoken in detail about product-based management. The most typical approach of product-based management is the system organized by operational units. Because you subdivide by type of product within the operational units, you need to manage by groups of products.

These groups are referred to as SBUs (strategic business units). Strategic management involves analysis of the long-term market by type of products and strategic planning for long-term business operations. Thus, in order to implement strategic management, it is very important to have product-based management.

This means that a long-term operational plan is translated into an annual plan; furthermore, it is reflected in the long-term plan for the company as a whole, which in turn becomes the basis for the mid- and long-term plans for each product and its annual plan.

If departmental or functional management, cross-functional management, and product-based management were carried out without reference to each other, utter confusion would result.

In other words, if the policies for the departments are set first, followed by the policies for the different functions, and there are discrepancies, the policies of the manufacturing section chief, written under the guidance of the department head, would come into conflict with the cross-functional policies. To avoid such a situation, set the cross-functional policies first, and then the policies for the different products. The policies for each department would then be set in response to the latter.

However, this cannot be accomplished in a single step. You start with policy deployment at the departmental levels, then go to daily management.

Koura: In policy deployment, tactics are generally formulated on an annual basis. But because results do not show up for two to three years, there are virtually no intermediate outcomes to check. Thus, for some time, only *do* (of the PDCA cycle) would be involved, creating the problem of what to do with evaluation. This is quite common in plans for research development.

Akao: The same is true of product-based management. You must approach it from the point of view of mid- or long-term plans. A short-term perspective would not do.

Koura: The issue is how to do this and organize the policy deployment schemes.

Importance of the QC Approach

Nomi: Today we discussed the important points of policy deployment. I am sure the readers will benefit from them, too. I learned many things, such as the idea that PDCA constitutes the foundation of policy deployment but that it becomes much more realistic if reversed to CAPD. In any case, the special feature of policy deployment is QC problem solving, and for that it is necessary to look not only at outcomes but at processes as well. It is imperative to recognize that policy deployment is a part of TQM and thus to use QC. Moreover, you must adapt the approach to the real conditions of your own company, coordinating it closely with the company's daily operations. At this point, I would like to have each of you give us your final summary.

Akao: Going back to the beginning, policy deployment is an integral part of TQM, and a mere verbal commitment is not enough. It must be implemented from the perspective of quality control. The methodology of QC must be employed, appropriate data collected, causal factors correctly identified, and actions taken on the basis of analysis.

Koura: As Mr. Akao says, there are structures and arrangement. When a company introduces policy deployment from a TQM perspective, there must be some kind of arrangement for it. For example, as reported in 1985, Komatsu formulated its own principles of policy deployment, which are shared by all Komatsu affiliates. To copy them would be to invite formalism, but Komatsu has a unique set. For example, CA is implemented in the form of a request for tasks to be undertaken. Ideally, each company should come up with its own arrangements or structures. (See Table 2-6.)

A certain company places much emphasis on the role of the president. When, in formulating targets and means, an argument arises as to whether to emphasize effectiveness or feasibility, the subordinates tend to view the matter from the point of view of feasibility. They might argue that the target is not achievable. While such attitudes need to be adjusted, ultimately the emphasis should be on the needs of the company, with policies formulated accordingly.

Another point has to do with the problem of priorities. To quote T. Sugimoto in "Quality Control of Clerical, Business, and Service Sectors": "We can talk about effectiveness and efficiency. As for which takes precedence, we would select something that is effective and seek efficiency in carrying that out. It would be a waste of time to take something that is ineffective and try to do it efficiently. The president of one company has made this principle the guide to formulating targets and means in the context of policy deployment. He ordered that the numerous means listed be reorganized accordingly.

Akao: In recent years, many companies have implemented TQM simply for the purpose of surviving. They recognize the need to build a business structure that can withstand changes in the environment.

Koura: We might call this the fundamental aim of policy deployment.

Akao: Policy deployment itself must be strengthened by the activities under it to be able to adjust to changes. This means that we must study QC all along.

Koura: In the end, we must recognize that the backbone of policy deployment is TQM. Policy deployment without TQM is useless.

Nomi: Thank you all for your participation.

Appendix 1
History of *Hoshin Kanri*

The Impetus to Systematize *Hoshin Kanri*

In 1962 the Bridgestone Tire Company conceived the idea of systematizing *hoshin kanri* as a part of TQC. The decision was occasioned by the company's investigation of companies that had won the Deming or Jisshi (application) prize. TQC (total quality control, or companywide quality control) was just being introduced then. At the same time, for the first time since World War II, Japan was being asked by the advanced countries to open up its markets. (Japan, feeling intense pressure, referred to the episode as the "second black-ship incident.")

In the 1960s, during the age of trade liberalization, many who ran Japan's businesses expressed concern as to whether they could survive in the face of an influx of technologically advanced products from the West and the cheap products from the developing countries, not to mention the keen domestic competition. It was in response to this underlying sense of crisis that systems such as TQC, *hoshin kanri*, quality control, and QC circles were introduced and developed. The establishment of the Deming Prize furthered these developments.

During the same decade, reviewers for the Deming Prize evaluated the application of SQC (statistical quality control) to the production and marketing (or servicing) of goods that meet the buyers' demands. To disseminate the practice of quality control, they pointed out problems related to *hoshin kanri*. What impressed the Bridgestone Tire representatives visiting prize-winning companies was the companies' attentiveness to issues related to *hoshin kanri* as a result of the competition review. The representatives came away convinced that they could develop an approach to TQC, thus bringing reform in management that would rise to the challenges of a turbulent period of internationalization. They sought to do this by systematizing and institutionalizing *hoshin kanri*, which was then being practiced piecemeal (e.g., through the establishment and development of policies and plans as management items).

This experience served as the springboard to a systematization of the then-disparate hoshin elements. Appendix Table 1-1 outlines the problems discovered and improvements made at Bridgestone Tire during this process.

Appendix Table 1-1. Problems and Improvements in *Hoshin Kanri* (Bridgestone Tire)

	Problems	Improvements
Formulating Policies and Plans	Policies and plans are conveyed orally or by memos. • The form and content of policies are unclear. • Policies are viewed as secret; hence, they tend to die out.	Write out policies and plans, and standardized forms. Must items: • Goals (quantified) • Measures (means of goal-attainment) Related items (related to 5WIH): • Background • Policies of the top management (main points) • Allocation of responsibilities • Schedule, etc.

	Determination, review, and analysis of previous year's performance are insufficient.
	• Goals (in quantitative terms) tend not to be specified.
	• There is emphasis on goals (expected results) and virtual neglect of process (how things are done).
	• The basis for measure is ambiguous; hence, measures tend to be ad hoc or based don KKD (*kan, keiken, dokyo,* or intuition, experience, and guts).
		Adopt the QC review process in its entirety.
		• Collect data and analyze the previous year's performance.
		• Use QC methods to solve problems.
		  Use problem-solving methods.
		  Use QC methods.
		• Prepare a summary chart of important problems.
		• Prepare an analysis report

	There is inadequate coordination between supervisors and subordinates when policies and plans are being formed. • Policies are lacking in thoroughness. • Policies are lacking in consistency.	Improve coordination of supervisors and subordinates during formulation of policies and plans (by facilitating discussion and exchange of ideas).
	Policies and plans are no developed systematically and comprehensively. • There is little confidence between supervisors and subordinates; hence, policies tend to lack vertical consistency and are easily disrupted. • There is a thick wall between departments; hence, there is poor interdepartmental coordination and cooperation.	Systematize policies. • Institute management by department (for vertical consistency). • Institute cross-functional management (for horizontal linkages).
	Problem 5: There is a lack of policies regarding quality, or policies and plans related to the promotion of quality control tend to be too general, lacking concreteness and long-term perspective.	For the company's prosperity and improvements of its structure, do the following: • Set up and develop policies regarding quality. • Formulate policies and plans (long term and short term) for the promotion of quality control.
Establishment of Management Items	The criteria for checking performance are unclear and tend to be the privileged information of each manager.	Specify and write up management items. • Use quantitative expressions. • QC methodology (especially control charts). • Clarify each item: job specification, management items, standards of management, methods of management, and so on.

	Every manager (e.g., department head, section chief, subsection chief) uses the same criteria for checking performance. • The relationship between management items of different levels is unclear.	Prepare a chart summarizing the different management items. • Specify management items by positions. • Bring together those in different positions when policies and plans are formulated.
	Measures to deal with unexpected situations are vague.	Prepare a document outlining how to deal with un-expected situations and how to initiate countermeasures (especially the analysis of causes, what measures to take, and how to put a brake on the situation)
Long-term Management Planning, Management Strategies, and Company Policies	Long-term vision on how to set the company's overall direction and adapt to change is weak. This weakness is especially apparent in the • collection and analysis of information • grasp of important problems • establishment of management strategies • setting of long-term goals • emphasis on financial planning (adding up of detailed accounts figures) • Company's relationship to annual policies and plans	Implement long-term (five-year) strategic planning. Incorporate into long-term management planning the following conditions: • Explicit long-term goals that indicate the company's future direction • A master plan • A creative and strategic management plan that can be used to predict risks and determine growth opportunities. • Resiliency • A "top-down" approach
	There is no long-term policy regarding quality and plans as part of the promotion of quality control.	Set long-term policies and plans, addressing quality and promotion of QC.
	The company's philosophy and principles of manage-ment are unclear.	Promulgate the company philosophy (or its basic principles of management). • Make explicit the spiritual base for the company's prosperity — its social responsibility.
System of Total Management	The system of management aimed at enhancing the strength of total involvement is unclear.	Establish a total management system. • Clarify the definition of a total management system and develop such a system
	There is a lack of formal rules and routes for trans-mitting, implementing, and gaining thorough acceptance of top-level policies • Information concerning policies is hard to get • There is a wide discrepancy in the ways policies are made known or received.	Establish a *hoshin kanri* system. • Actively adopt *hoshin kanri* as a means of imple-menting a system of total management • Aim toward establishment of a system of quality assurance based on the idea that quality in the market is top priority.
Diagnosis and Evaluation	Methods of checking TQC activities, including the development of policies and their implementation, are not clearly understood.	Implement QC diagnosis, or assessment: • For example, diagnosis by the president, diagnosis by the department heads
	There is a lack of clarity as to how to evaluate policies and actual management	Systemize the evaluation of *hoshin kanri*.

Arnold J. Toynbee (1889-1975) noted that no civilization was ever destroyed by external enemies. The downfall of the Roman Empire, for example, was its inner decay and disunity. *Hoshin kanri* is based on this principle, too. It is a means to pull together the forces within a company and to unite the minds internally (coordinate the vectors), to perpetually improve its performance by adjusting quickly to changes.

Relationship between *Hoshin Kanri* and Target Control

Any discussion of *hoshin kanri* (also called policy deployment or management by policy) must include mention of its relationship to management by objectives. The first half of the 1960s was a period in which management by objectives rapidly gained favor among many companies in both the United States and Japan.

The concept of management by objectives was introduced by Peter Drucker in his book *The Practice of Management* (1954). A number of behavioral scientists took up the concept, furnishing it with a theoretical basis and methods of application for managers and administrators. For example, the "XY theory" of Douglas MacGregor is widely known as the theoretical underpinning to management by objectives. And Edward C. Schleh's book, *Management by Results* (1962), played an important role in disseminating the concept of management by objectives. Even in Japan, the latter half of the 1960s saw a rapid spread in use of management by objectives.

Management by objectives was created and promoted aggressively as a means to overcome the difficulties American businesses faced in the 1950s as a result of a slumping economy and an intensification of competition. Thus, both *hoshin kanri* and management by objectives can be regarded as products of their times, each responding to the specific needs of those times.

While ideas for systematizing *hoshin kanri* as part of TQC were still being shaped, it was suggested that the new approach be labeled "management by results" since Schleh, an authority on the concept, had published a book by that title in 1964 emphasizing the same principles. The suggestion was rejected, however, for the following reasons:

1. The term *results* as used by Schleh refers to "expected results" and as such to objectives. The implied notion of "layout" *(waritsuke)* also carries a significant meaning. In TQC, however, process is emphasized, as in the phrase "process more than results." Further, the concept of "management" is more important

than that of "layout" or "control." The translated term of *management by results* could therefore be misleading.

2. It was deemed necessary to establish a unique, comprehensive system that would incorporate the advantages of management by objectives while becoming a part of TQC (see Appendix Table 1-2).

As a result of the evaluation, the tentative term *policy management* was introduced in the TQC Promotional Plan of December 1964. In February and March 1965, the label *hoshin kanri* was made official and the system put into practice. In the spring of that year, the system was introduced in the company by-laws and in July it was written up as "Outline of *Hoshin Kanri*" (to be later incorporated into company regulations as "Regulations Concerning Policy Deployment").

Appendix Table 1-2. Comparison of *Hoshin Kanri* and Management by Objectives

Similarities
1. Aim: Prosperity of the company (attainment of goals and improvement of performance)
2. Self-determination of goals and self-evaluation of the results of implementation
3. In setting of continuously higher goals: • Intensification of goals • Implementation of coordination, discussion, and exchange of ideas • Efforts by subordinates to set and attain goals beyond their capabilities • Inducement of creativity and improvement of morale
Differences (special features of *hoshin kanri*)
1. QC solutions to important problems (emphasis on process) • Grasp of problems • Utilization of QC attitude and methods • Application of QC procedures in solving problems
2. Formulation of management items
3. Establishment and implementation of a system of total quality management • Focus on *hoshin kanri* and aim for the establishment of a system of quality assurance • Emphasis on sale of products that meet consumer demand, are of high quality, and ultimately serve society This is desirable so long as the autonomy of the QC circles is preserved.
Note. The points listed under "Differences" are based on surveys and studies dealing with the Bridgestone Tire Company.

Relationship between *Hoshin Kanri* and QC Circles

Recently we are often asked, Is it necessary to implement policy deployment in QC circles, too? The answer is no.

1. *Hoshin kanri* is targeted for the company officers and department and section chiefs. (In some companies senior supervisors are included).
2. The special feature of QC circles is self-management. Therefore, the selection of topics for discussion in QC circles and their solutions should be left to the workers' initiative. Hoshin planning should not be imposed on them as compulsory.
3. Once the activities of the QC circles become regularized, communication with the members of management is likely to increase and become smooth, thereby increasing the chances of learning about the themes (or tasks) taken up by the management. The QC circles would sometimes select the same (or similar) themes as the management.

Appendix Figure 1-1 shows the basic relationship between *hoshin kanri* (introduced in 1965) and QC circle activities (initiated in 1962-63).

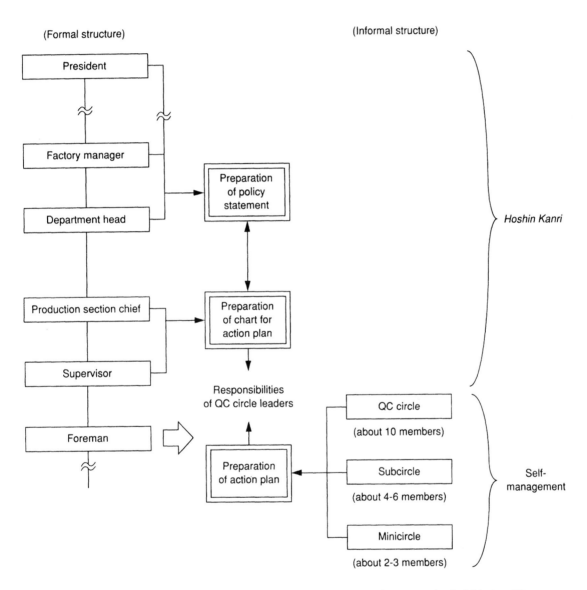

(Formal structure)　　　　　　　　　　　　　　　(Informal structure)

President

Factory manager

Department head → Preparation of policy statement

Production section chief → Preparation of chart for action plan

Supervisor

Responsibilities of QC circle leaders

Foreman → Preparation of action plan

Hoshin Kanri

QC circle (about 10 members)

Subcircle (about 4-6 members)

Minicircle (about 2-3 members)

Self-management

QC circle activities are based on autonomy, creativity, teamwork, and the freedom to exercise individual qualities.

Appendix Figure 1-1. *Hoshin Kanri* **and QC Circle Activities**

Appendix 2
Chronology of *Hoshin Kanri*

The development of *hoshin kanri* is summarized in Appendix Tables 2-1 and 2-2. Appendix Table 2-1 covers the period from 1950 to 1969, when both *hoshin kanri* and quality control were developed. Appendix Table 2-2 covers the period between 1970 and 1988, during which time *hoshin kanri* spread rapidly and matured. For this reason, Appendix Table 2-2 focuses on the development of *hoshin kanri* alone.

Appendix Table 2-1. History of *Hoshin Kanri* and Management by Objectives (1950-69)

Year	*Hoshin Kanri*	Management by Objectives
	1950-59	
1950	Japan Association of Science and Technology sponsors an eight-day course on QC with Dr. Deming as guest. • Serves as impetus for dissemination of Deming Cycle and PDCA management cycle • Forms the basis of *hoshin kanri*	
1951	Establishment of the Deming Prize • Emphasis on policies and plans to introduce and promote QC on a companywide basis • Inclusion of such emphasis in statement of award • *Hoshin kanri* listed as main criterion in the evaluation for the Deming Prize	
1954	Japan Association of Science and Technology holds seminar on QC with Dr. Juran as guest (for directors, department and section chiefs) • Triggered shift in Japan's QC from emphasis on SQC to emphasis on management • Pointed out director's responsibility to take action in accordance with company's QC plans, criteria, and goals	Peter Drucker's *The Practice of Management*, in which management by objectives was proposed, is published in Japanese. • Drucker's system of management by objectives emphasizes stages of management • GM's divisional system draws attention in Japan
1955	Kayano Ken publishes "Managers and Quality Control," in which he stresses need for managers to set and implement policies based on quality and quality control.	Management by objectives is practiced widely in the U.S. from the second half of the 1950s into the 1960s. A growing number of companies adopt the system in order to ride out the business slump and growing competition of the 1950s.
1956	Plans formulated after receipt of Deming Prize begin to emphasize total quality control and companywide quality control.	
1957	Dr. Ishikawa Kaoru and associates publish their views on importance of management and operational policies. Relationship between the two intensifies.	Several companies in Japan (Nippon Glass, for example) adopt and implement management by objectives.
1958	The term *total quality control* appears for the first time in a statement of the Deming Prize award, emphasizing the importance of making long-term plans following receipt of the award.	

Year	*Hoshin Kanri*	Management by Objectives
	1960-69	
1960	The journal *Hinshitsu Kanri* (Quality Control) publishes a year-long series, "TQC Seminar: Quality Control for Everyone." • Policy issues are discussed. • Articles on trade liberalization appear with increasing frequency. • Appearing in award statements are terms such as *management, management policy, long-term management planning,* and *total planning.* Dr. Juran lectures on general management emphasizing the nature of management, the responsibilities of managers, the setting of goals, general planning and planning for improvement. These lectures are to influence the development of *hoshin kanri.*	Theoretical underpinning is established by a group of behavorial scientists in the first half of 1960s; management by objectives is thus systematized and prepared for wide use. • The theorists include McGregor, Likert, Schleh, Blake, Maslow, McConaughy, and Ardris. • Some of their influential works are *The Human Side of Enterprise* (1960; translated to Japanese in 1966) and *New Patterns of Management* (1961; translated to Japanese in 1964.)
1961	Companies winning the Deming Prize make statements emphasizing companywide quality control, total management, long-term management planning, quality control, basic policy, management for profits, management items, grasp of important problems, and other building blocks of *hoshin kanri.* • Teijin's summary chart of management items (by function) and Nippon Denso's orientation toward a total management system formed the basis of *hoshin kanri* as it developed. • Deming Prize winner Kato Takeo speaks about the need to establish, develop, and implement management and policies based on quality and quality control.	Schleh's book *Management by Results* is published. This work greatly facilitates the dissemination of management by objectives in Japan and the United States. • Schleh greatly advanced Drucker's theory and methods. He promoted in practical terms the implementation of policy not only at the top level but also at the bottom level. • Schleh uses the term *results* to mean "results expected in the future," "goals."
1962	Advances are made in organization by function and cross-functional management (Sumitomo Denko).	Schleh's ideas and methods of management by objectives are introduced in Japan and adopted by a few pioneering companies (such as Teijin).
1963	Nippon Kaso promotes a total management system (company philosophy, long-term management planning, operation planning, prioritizing of problems, etc.) and especially the incorporation of checkpoints. Toyota publicly announces a top-level policy on the "organization of a cross-functional management system." Komatsu announces its "regulations on operations by function."	*Management by Results* is translated to Japanese (by Ueno Ichiro). This work sets off a boom in Japan in management by objectives.

Year	*Hoshin Kanri*	Management by Objectives
1960-69		
1963	Professor Ishikawa Kaoru emphasizes "strengthening daily management" in his article "Reflecting on the Second Conference on QC for Front-Line Supervisors" (in Genba to QC Shi).	
1964	Komatsu Manufacturing appointed a manager to take charge of cross-functional management. Komatsu clarifies total management and quality assurance, and introduces the flag method. • The flag method is still regarded as an excellent way to develop goals. Bridgestone Tire introduces the term *hoshin kanri* based on its studies and trials.	Management by objectives is seriously adopted in Japan: • Sumitomo Kinzoku Kozan and Jujo Seishi, among others, took pioneering leadership roles. • Sumitomo Kinzoku Kozan became a devotee of Drucker's ideas and led the way in adopting management by objectives.
1965	Toyota develops systematized policies, policy management, cross-functional management, and other management concepts. Professor Akao defines "items of daily management" in his article "Concerning the Setting of Goals and Policies in Cross-Functional Management" (*Hinshitsu Kanri Shi)* Bridgestone Tire codifies the principles of *hoshin kanri* based on a compilation of its own and other companies' studies and experiences.	Management by objectives is widely adopted in Japan in the second half of the 1960s: • The economic recession of 1964-65 spurred this boom. • Ueno Ichiro published his *Mokuhyo Ni Yoru Kanri* (Management by objectives) and thereby contributed greatly to dissemination of management by objectives. • Denden Kosha, Toshiba, Hamano Textiles, and other companies introduced and implemented management by objectives across the board and with originality.
1966	Matsushita's products department develops an important model of *hoshin kanri* through its systematization of management, annual operational planning, and establishment of a center for cost management.	
1968	In its report on the promotion of TQC, Bridgestone Tire outlines a method to develop *hoshin kanri* and establish a quality assurance system for the purpose of management reform.	Management by objectives hit a plateau in Japan after the rapid diffusion up to 1970. It continues to find favor, however, in companies seeking to modernize management. Furthermore, the system is widely accepted in Western Europe, the communist bloc, and developing countries.

Appendix Table 2-2. History of *Hoshin Kanri*

1970-79	
1970	Professor Asaka Tetsuichi, in this special lecture at the National Conference on QC titled "Quality Control in Planning," emphasizes the importance of planning based on review and on problem solving in the context of TQC (corresponding to the main points of *hoshin kanri*). Naruge Shuichi publishes *Ningensei Shiko* (Toward Humanness), which wins the quality control literature prize awarded by Nikkei. The book reports on the meaning and status of strategic planning and *hoshin kanri*. An increasing number of companies adopt and use cross-functional management (focused on the function of quality assurance) and *hoshin kanri*.
1975-76	The term *hoshin kanri* (policy deployment) becomes widely accepted. Pentel, Ishikawa-jima Harima Heavy Industries, and other companies adopt and use the companywide control chart for *hoshin kanri*. Professor Koura Takazo, in his article "Past and Present Status of Ideas on Management Items," distinguishes between management items of departmental and functional management and those within the QC plan of operations (later referred to as "items of daily management"). Special editions of *Hinshitsu Kanri Shi* are planned and developed to cover topics related to *hoshin kanri*. Articles such as "How to Formulate Quality Control Policies" (October 1976), "How to Make a QC Diagnosis" (December 1978), and "*Hoshin Kanri*" (December 1979) are among them.
1980-89	
1981	Professor Asaka Tetsuichi, in his special lecture "Riding Out Difficult Times with TQC," delivered at the 15th National QC Conference, emphasizes the importance of establishing management strategies (especially operational strategies). The Japan Association of Quality Control Specialists holds a symposium on *hoshin kanri* under TQC. A systematic explanation of terms and concepts in *hoshin kanri* appears in "Management Items and Hoshin Kanri for Department and Section Heads" (*Hinshitsu Gekkan* 128), edited by Professor Yoji Akao. (In it, Kobayashi Kosei's target-means matrix is cited as an example.)
1988	Nippon Kikaku Kyokai (Japan Association of Standards) publishes a series of works focusing on *hoshin kanri*. Examples are "Discussion of *Hoshin Kanri*," "Quality Control Practices," "Cross-functional Management Practices," and "*Hoshin Kanri* Practices."

Appendix 3
Management Strategies

The Era of Strategic Management

The American-style practice of long-term management planning was adopted by Japanese businesses early in the postwar period. Long-term planning (normally, a five-year plan) as developed in Japan diffused rapidly beginning around 1955 as a means to modernize management; by 1963 nearly 70 percent of the nation's principal businesses had adopted the practice. It was during this period that *hoshin kanri* as a part of TQC was formulated and began to be systematized.

Systematization of Total Management

The postwar period was a time when businesses aimed to establish and develop management strategies, as Japan was then being pressed to open her market (in particular, to liberalize her trade). This was referred to as the "second black ship incident." The Nippon Kayaku Company developed the framework for long-term planning and annual operational planning as part of strategic planning, having been introduced to these ideas when it was awarded the Deming Prize in 1963 (see Appendix Figure 3-1). As the principles of strategic management permeated the entire company as part of company philosophy (or its basic management principles), advances were made in organizing a comprehensive management system based on annual policies and plans and annual budgets within the context of long-term management planning. Management strategy then consisted of a three-pronged growth strategy, riding on a tide of high economic growth, with marketing strategy at the core: "share up," "morale up," and "cost up."

The Decline of Long-term Management Planning

As the systematization of a total management structure advanced, a problem developed based on long-term planning strategies of the 1960s. The problem had to do with the professionalization of the budgetary process (involving financial or cumulative mathematical programming procedures). It affected the formulation of

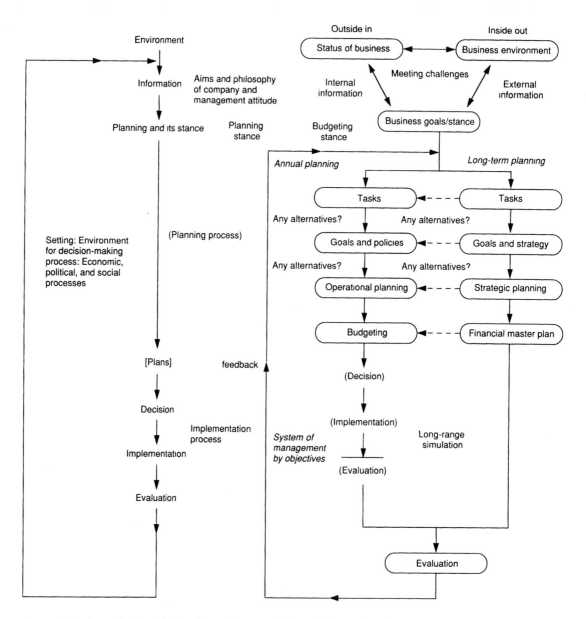

Appendix Figure 3-1. Model for Long-term and Annual Operational Planning (Nippon Kayaku)

long-term planning as well as the formulation of annual policies and plans. The accompanying formalization takes place especially in the following situations:

- When the coordination of long-term management planning with annual policies and plans and budgets becomes formalistic

- When an effort is made to have the first-year plan under long-term planning (t-year) agree with the year's budget (in the case of important items, with the annual policies and plans as well)
- When the division in charge of budgeting fails to also take full responsibility for *hoshin kanri* (policy deployment)

The above situations are most likely to arise when long-term planning is carried out with an emphasis on numbers focused on plans for profits and quantitative analysis. This kind of long-term planning strategy met its demise in August 1981, when Japan suffered the so-called Nixon shock (the adjustment to Nixon's policy to protect a dollar that was chronically weakening throughout the 1960s, bringing about international uncertainty surrounding the currencies of nations; and to the shift from a fixed to a floating exchange rate system, whereby the fixed rate of 360 yen to the dollar crumbled to 308 yen).

The problem was that long-term planning based on mathematical programming was too rigid to adjust itself to such dramatic changes and therefore became obsolete. Many companies gave up long-term planning during this period. In such circumstances even a good strategic plan would be separated from long-term planning and not be utilized.

Long-term Management Planning that Can Adapt to Change

Japan's economy was plunged into a slow-growth period following the added blow of the first oil crisis (commonly referred to as the "oil shock"), which came in the aftermath of the "Nixon shock." There thus arose the demand for a long-term planning strategy that could adapt quickly to changes. An answer to that demand came in Naruge Shuichi's book *Ningen Shiko* (Toward Humanness), which emphasized the philosophy of management from a manager's perspective and received an award in 1970 for the best work on quality control.

The Process and System of Formulating a Strategic Long-term Plan

The important elements in formulating a long-term management planning system are outlined below:

1. Long-term management planning must be *goal-oriented*. It is meaningless to evaluate a plan only in terms of whether a numerical target was attained or not. Forecasting is nothing more than a framework for planning. To plan is to anticipate problems that a company is likely to face in the context of this framework and to consider what needs to be done to solve them. At the same

Appendix Table 3-1. Management Tasks from a Strategic Point of View

Type of Management		Definition
Traditional	(1) Drifting management	Premodern management style in which ad hoc measures are adopted as problems arise
	(2) Tactical management	Management system under which there is systematic management with measures adopted being tactically most suited to the specific environmental conditions
Strategic	(3) Quasi-strategic management	Management system in which there is awareness of need and readiness to adopt to environmental changes but also a lack of experience in making tactical choices.
	(4) Strategic management	Management system in which changes in the environment are foreseen and actions are taken accordingly.

time, a manager needs to go beyond problem solving and to cultivate new opportunities by actively taking advantage of the company's strong points.

In this sense, when dealing with quantitative targets such as amount of sales, it is necessary to recognize clearly whether one is talking about a forecast or a goal. Only by making these distinctions clearly can there be any formulation of policies in terms of what needs to be done.

2. Long-term management planning must be holistic in character, that is, not only long-term but wide-ranging. In other words, it must be a master plan that determines the most appropriate target for each department from the perspective of the company as a whole. The individual plans of the departments must be coordinated and evaluated from a companywide perspective and organized into a master plan.

3. Long-term management planning must include a strategic element.

4. Long-term management planning must avoid rigidity and be resilient.

5. Long-term management planning must have as its basis a top-down approach.

Long-term Management Planning Based on a Top-down Format

Long-term management planning varies depending on the leadership ability and attitude of the managers. Three types of managers are desirable. Professor H.

Igor Ansoff, known for his work on the theory of strategic management and long-term planning, distinguishes the three types as follows:

1. The *responsive* type: waits for problems to actually occur rather than actively seeking solutions to impending problems or threats (crises)
2. The *planner* type: anticipates problems and comes up with ways to avoid them
3. The *entrepreneur* type: anticipates both problems and opportunities and deals with them beforehand.

The *entrepreneur* type is best suited to formulating and implementing strategic long-term planning and to seeking growth of the enterprise. He or she is in constant pursuit of strategic opportunities and actively seeks to adapt to changes, not content to simply anticipate and deal with crises.

The Formulation of Long-term Management Plans Based on a QC Perspective

In planning management strategy it is important to formulate as a tool long-term management planning from a QC perspective. Its process and system are summarized in Appendix Figures 3-2 and 3-3.

The Rise of Strategic Management

Professor Nakamura Motoichi (Asia University) has commented that the 1980s was a period of turbulence brought on by the intensity and rapidity of changes in the environment. He has argued the need for strategic management, reasoning that without it businesses can neither prosper nor survive.

"Strategic planning" was conceived by a group of Western businesses in the mid-1960s. It wasn't until the mid-1970s, however, that the idea was adopted in Japan, first by large, progressive companies. The term *strategic management* came into wide use during the 1980s, when many American businesses and Japan's more progressive businesses adopted the approach.

What is strategic management? Kogure Masao (Tokyo Kogyo University and Tamagawa University) explains the role of TQC within strategic management in his book *TQC To Senrayaku Keiei* (TQC and strategic management).

According to Kogure, management (here used to refer to the management system) is classified and defined according to the status of management strategy (Appendix Table 3-1). Even in strategic management, it is necessary for the managers to be immersed deeply in TQC so that they can concentrate on carrying out fully what they are expected to in terms of strategic activities (aggressive management, aggressive action based on QC).

Structure of task allocation

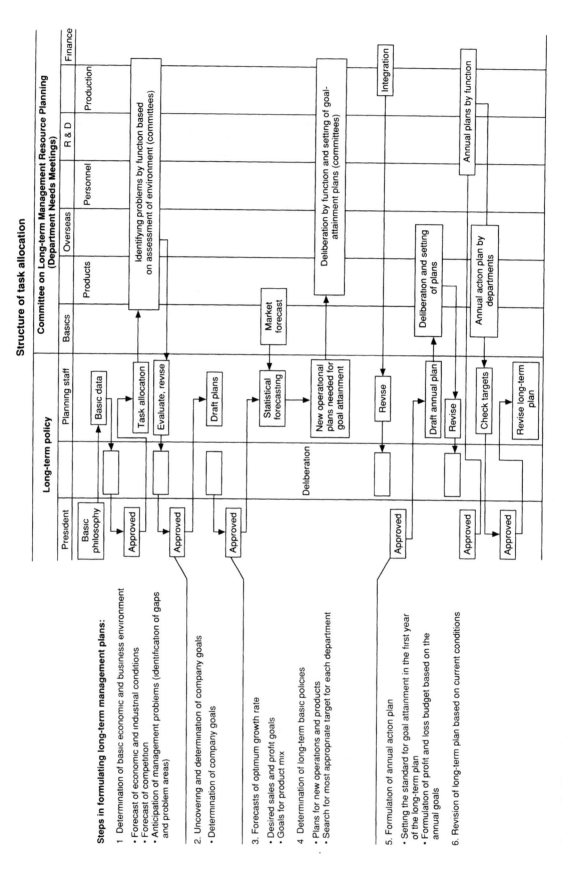

Steps in formulating long-term management plans:

1 Determination of basic economic and business environment
- Forecast of economic and industrial conditions
- Forecast of competition
- Anticipation of management problems (identification of gaps and problem areas)

2. Uncovering and determination of company goals
- Determination of company goals

3. Forecasts of optimum growth rate
- Desired sales and profit goals
- Goals for product mix

4. Determination of long-term basic policies
- Plans for new operations and products
- Search for most appropriate target for each department

5. Formulation of annual action plan
- Setting the standard for goal attainment in the first year of the long-term plan
- Formulation of profit and loss budget based on the annual goals

6. Revision of long-term plan based on current conditions

Appendix Figure 3-2. The Process of Formulating Long-term Management Plans: A Model

Committee on Long-term Management Resource Planning and Policies:

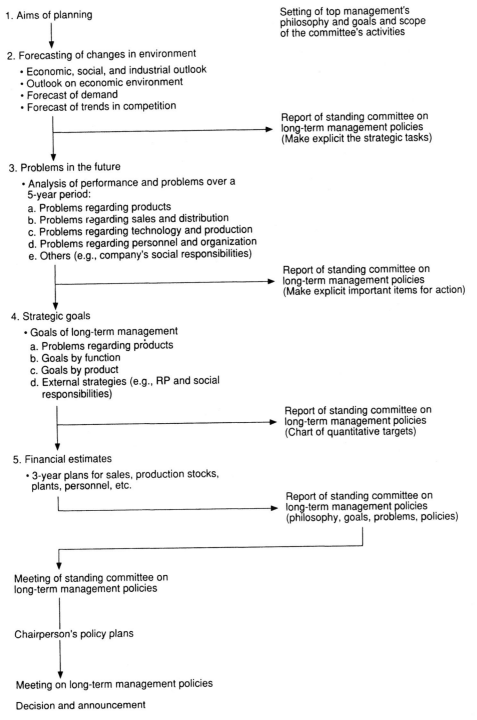

1. Aims of planning

Setting of top management's philosophy and goals and scope of the committee's activities

2. Forecasting of changes in environment

- Economic, social, and industrial outlook
- Outlook on economic environment
- Forecast of demand
- Forecast of trends in competition

Report of standing committee on long-term management policies (Make explicit the strategic tasks)

3. Problems in the future

- Analysis of performance and problems over a 5-year period:
  a. Problems regarding products
  b. Problems regarding sales and distribution
  c. Problems regarding technology and production
  d. Problems regarding personnel and organization
  e. Others (e.g., company's social responsibilities)

Report of standing committee on long-term management policies (Make explicit important items for action)

4. Strategic goals

- Goals of long-term management
  a. Problems regarding products
  b. Goals by function
  c. Goals by product
  d. External strategies (e.g., RP and social responsibilities)

Report of standing committee on long-term management policies (Chart of quantitative targets)

5. Financial estimates

- 3-year plans for sales, production stocks, plants, personnel, etc.

Report of standing committee on long-term management policies (philosophy, goals, problems, policies)

Meeting of standing committee on long-term management policies

Chairperson's policy plans

Meeting on long-term management policies

Decision and announcement

Appendix Figure 3-3. A System for Setting Long-term Management Policies

Relationship of *Hoshin Kanri* to Budget Management

In many cases companies have retained traditional systems of budget management after *hoshin kanri* has been implemented. Worse, some companies have held to old budget-management practices at the expense of true *hoshin kanri*. In fact, the reverse should be true: You need to establish *hoshin kanri* as the overall system and adapt budget management accordingly (Appendix Figure 3-4).

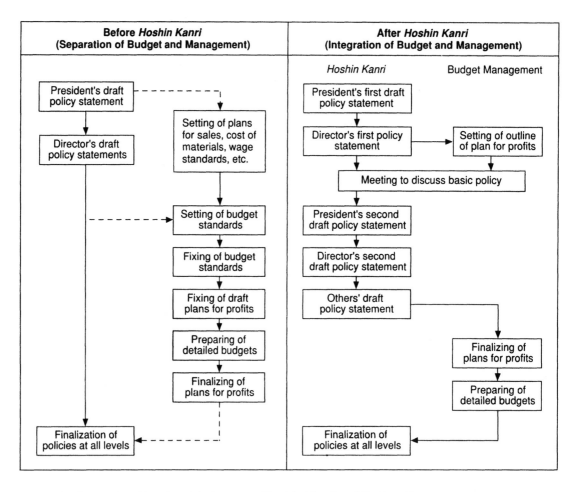

Appendix Figure 3-4. Relationship between *Hoshin Kanri* and Budget Management

Bibliography

Akao, Yoji. 1964. On inspection, control, and evaluation points. *QC* (special spring supplement on Matsuyama QC Conference Papers) 15: 42-48 (in Japanese).

_____. 1965. Role of control points in overall control system. *Standardization and QC* 18 (no. 10): 1-10 (in Japanese).

_____. 1965. Setup of target policy for functional control. *QC* (special spring supplement): 525, 532 (in Japanese).

_____. 1967. Role of control points in target control. *Standardization and QC* 20 (no. 8, 12): 6-14, 23 (in Japanese).

_____. 1980. Target deployment and plan deployment. *QC* 31 (May, special supplement): 63-67 (in Japanese).

_____. 1982. Organization and administration for companywide QC. *Organizational science* 16: 42-50 (in Japanese).

_____. 1984. Target and means deployment and set-up of control point. *Quality* 14 (no. 1): 28-36 (in Japanese).

_____. 1984. TQC and hoshin kanri. *Standardization and QC* 27 (no. 6): 2-6 (in Japanese).

Akao, Yoji, ed. 1981. Control: Management items and hoshin kanri for department and section heads. *Hinshitsu gekkan* (QC monthly) 128 (October):1-11, 22-34.

Akao, Yoji, and Yuichi Iijima. 1965. Setting of goals and policies in cross-functional management. *Hinshitsu kanri* (QC) (special spring supplement) 16: 109-20.

Akao, Yoji, Kozo Koura, and Tokisuke Nomi. 1984. Special edition: Why hoshin kanri now? *Hyojunka to hinshitsu kanri* 37, no. 6.

Akao, Yoji, et al. 1984. Proceedings of the sixteenth symposium on cross-functional management. Nippon Hinshitsu Gakkai.

Akao, Yoji, Hideo Nojiri, and Naoyuki Shiga. 1985. Hoshin kanri and operational plans. *Hinshitsu kanri* (QC) (special May supplement) 36: 74-77.

Akao, Yoji, K. Miura, and T. Nomi. 1986. Hoshin kanri as a part of TQC. *Standardization and QC*, no. 12, p. 23 (in Japanese).

Akao, Yoji, Nomi Tokisuke, and Koura Kozo. 1988. *Hoshin kanri katsuyo no jissai* (Hoshin kanri practices). Nippon Kikaku Kyokai.

Aoki, Shigeru. 1981. Cross-functional management for top management. *Hinshitsu kanri* 32 (nos. 2-4).

Asada, K. 1965. Control method of kobe plant (no. 1). *QC* 16 (special fall supplement): 1-4 (in Japanese).

Asaka, Tetsuichi. 1981. Quality control for planning. *Hyojunka to hinshitsu kanri* 23 (no. 8).

_____. 1981. Riding through difficult times with TQC. *Hyojunka to hinshitsu kanri* 34 (no. 8): 13-23.

Asaka, Tetsuichi. 1981. *TQC no kihon* (Foundation of TQC). Nippon Kikaku Kyokai.

Asaka, Tetsuichi, et al. 1987. Special edition: QC diagnosis. *Hyojunka to hinshitsu kanri* 40 (no. 2): 4-38.

Comany Co. 1985. 1985 Deming Award, Japan QC Award, Speech on Award Presentation, Comany Co.: 9 (in Japanese).

Control Engineering Department. 1967 Deming Plan Department, Bridgestone Co. *QC* 18 (no. 12):59-61 (in Japanese).

Deming Prize Committee. Summary of special lectures given on receipt of the Deming Prize. Nippon Kagakugijutsu Renmei (hereafter abbreviated as Nikka Giren).

Drucker, Peter F. 1954. *The practice of management.* New York: Harper and Brothers.

_____. 1987. *Gendai keiei kenkyu kai* (Current management/top management techniques and examples). 2 vols. Translated from English by Nodo Kazuo. Jiyukokumin-sha.

Fujita Kaoru, et al. 1978. Seminar series: How to make QC diagnosis. *Hinshitsu kanri* 29: (nos. 1-12).

Gakken-Sangyo Kyoiku Jigyo Kai, ed. 1979. Know-how of group administration. Pt. 2: 146-58 (in Japanese).

Hara, K., and H. Shiramura. 1965. An example of QC for the casting industry. *QC* (special spring supplement): 462-466 (in Japanese).

Hinshitsu Kanrishi. Editorial Board. 1962. TQC seminar: Quality control for everyone. *Hinshitsu kanri shi:* 12-14.

Hirose, K. 1986. QC circles of sales-service industries: Hoshin kanri promotion. *Quality monthly* (no. 175): 57 (in Japanese).

Hisazumi, K., and T. Tekko. 1982. Control items of department and section heads at Kobayashi-Kosei. *QC* 32 (no. 8): 23-37 (in Japanese).

Hosotani, Katsuya. 1984. *QC attitude and point of view.* Tokyo: JUSE (in Japanese).

_____. 1987. Hoshin kanri and daily management. Proceedings of the 44th QC symposium on special features and problems of Japan's QC (part 2). Tokyo: Nikka Giren.

Hosotani, Katsuya, et al. 1987. Seminar series: Hoshin kanri and daily management. *Hinshitsu kanri* 38: (nos. 7-12).

Iijima, A. 1981. Control items of department and section heads at Toyota Shatai. *QC* 32 (no. 8): 27-32 (in Japanese).

Ikezawa, Tatsuo, et al. 1979. Special edition: Hoshin kanri. *Hinshitsu kanri* 30 (no. 12).

Imai, T. 1986. Hoshin kanri for TQC. *Standardization and QC* 39 (no. 12): 37-45 (in Japanese).

Imaizumi, Ekisei. Hinshitsu kakumei (Quality revolution). *Hinshitsu gekkan* 109: 16-21.

Irie, I., ed. "Multinational Company Study Group Author (1985): International Management Risk Theory," p. 105, *Bunshindo* (original) Root, F.R. (1982), *Foreign market entry strategy*, New York: Amacom, 148, Fig. 14.

Ishibashi, M. (1952, 1969). Top Diagnosis of this Company: 9th QC Symposium Report, "Features and Problems of Japanese QC," JUSE, 177-191 (in Japanese).

Ishihara, H. 1977. *VE text on work floor.* Tokyo: Nikka Giren (in Japanese).

Ishihara, K. 1984. *Companywide QC promotion.* Tokyo: JUSE (in Japanese).

Ishihara, K., et al. 1970. QC policy, plan deployment, and staff's role. *QC* 21 (no. 11): 68-81 (in Japanese).

Ishikawa, Kaoru. 1963. Reflecting on the second QC conference for front-line supervisors. *Genba to QC* (no. 8): 2-6 (in Japanese).

_____. 1979. *New QC introduction.* Tokyo: JUSE 11 (in Japanese).

_____. 1981. Series seminar: TQC introduction, promotion, and cross-functional management. *QC* 32 (no. 11): 88-96 (in Japanese).

_____. 1986. *Japanese QC.* Tokyo: JUSE (in Japanese).

Ishikawa, Kaoru, ed. 1962. *Control charts* Tokyo: Nikka Giren.

Ishikawa, Kaoru, et al. 1956. QC seminar no. 9: Quality control. *Hinshitsu kanri* 8 (no. 10): 62-80.

Ishikawa, Kaoru, and T. Koura. 1979. *Control point of quality.* Zeimu-Keiri-Kyokai.

Jujikawa, K., et al. 1978. Series: Way of QC diagnosis. *QC* 29 (nos. 1-12) (in Japanese).

Juran, J.M. 1962. *General management*. Series of lectures given to directors and heads of departments and sections. Sponsored by Nikka Giren (in Japanese).

_____. 1969. *Management philosophy of breakthrough*. Tokyo: JUSE (in Japanese).

Kanazaki, I., K. Okada, and T. Wokabayashi. CD (cost down) movement based on overall control system. *QC* 17 (special spring supplement): 58-59 (in Japanese).

Kano, N. 1981. Daily control and its control items. 32 (no. 8):15-24 (in Japanese).

_____. 1983. Through daily control. *Quality monthly* 147: 19-21 (in Japanese).

Katayama, Z., et al. 1986. Functional control and standardization. *Standardization and QC* 39 (no. 8): 47-49 (in Japanese).

Kayano, Ken. 1955. QC Seminar: What should managers do? *Hinshitsu kanri* 6 (no. 4): 43-46.

Kitahata, N. 1964. Control of the work floor and the promotion status. *QC* (special issue on Matsuyama QC Conference Papers): 34-39 (in Japanese).

Koda, Kazuo. 1973. *Mokuhyo kanri no susumekata* (How to implement hoshin kanri). Tokyo: Sangyo Noritsu University Press (SANNO).

Kogure, Masao. 1984. *TQC to senryaku keiei* (TQC and strategic management). Tokyo: Nikka Giren.

Kogure, Masao, et al. 1983. Special edition: QC diagnosis by top management. *Hinshitsu kanri* 34 (no. 12).

Kono, Noriaki, ed. 1983. Importance of daily management. *Kanri gekkan:* 147.

Kono, Noriaki, Shioyama Hidemasa, and Takasu Hisashi. 1985. Daily management and TQC. No. 7 in seminar series on TQC. *Hinshitsu kanri* 36 (no. 7): 90-104.

Kono, Toyohiro, ed. 1978. *Saishin choki keiei keikaku no jisurei* (Examples of recent long-term management planning). Tokyo: Dobunkan.

Koura, Kozo. 1970. *QC of clerical work*. Tokyo: Nippon Kogyo Shimrun (in Japanese).

_____. 1978. Past and present status of ideas on management items. *Hinshitsu* 8 (no. 2): 9-16.

_____. 1987. Daily management. No. 2 in seminar series on hoshin kanri and daily management. *Hinshitsu kanri* 38 (no. 8).

Koura, Kozo, et al. 1986. Special edition: Cross-functional management and standardization. *Hyojunka to hinshitsu kanri* 39 (no. 8).

Kuimoyamada, K. 1984. Cross-functional management for QA. *Quality* 14 (no. 4): 63-69 (in Japanese).

Kume, Hitoshi, et al. 1982. Special edition: Issues in promoting hoshin kanri. *Hinshitsu kanri* 33 (no. 9).

Kurogane, Kenji, et al. 1988. *Kinobetsu kanri katsuyo no jissai* (Cross-functional management practices). Tokyo: Nippon Kikaku Kyokai.

Kusaba, I. 1964. On control items. *QC* 15 (special spring supplement): 55-57 (in Japanese).

_____. 1985. On the Deming Prize audit. *Quality control* 9 (no. 9): 15, 46 (in Japanese).

Likert, R. 1961. *New patterns of management.* New York: McGraw-Hill. Translated from English by Misumi Juji. 1964. *Keiei no kodokagau.* Tokyo: Daimondo-sha.

MacGregor, D. 1960. *The human side of enterprise.* New York: McGraw-Hill. Translated from English by Takahashi Tatsuo. 1966. *Kigyo no ningenteki sokumen.* Tokyo: Sangyo Noritsu College Press (SANNO).

Mizuno, S. 1984. *Companywide QC.* Tokyo: Nikka Giren (in Japanese).

Mizuno, S., ed. 1979. *QC method development group: Seven new QC tools for managers and staffs.* Tokyo: JUSE (in Japanese).

Mizuno, S., and Yoji Akao. 1978. *Quality function deployment.* Tokyo: JUSE (in Japanese).

Mizuno, S., et al. Control points: a panel discussion. 15 (no. 8): 34-36 (in Japanese).

Mochimoto, Shiko. 1985. *TQC mi yoru senryaku keiei no tenkai* (Development of strategic management under TQC). Tokyo: Nikka Giren.

Mochiyuki, S. 1986. Cross-functional management and QA. *Standardization & QC* 39 (no. 8): 13-20 (in Japanese).

Mori, H. 1986. TQC and strategy. Twentieth Q-S National Conference Papers. No. 1 subgroup orientation. Tokyo: Japan Standards Association (in Japanese).

Mura, K. 1984. Roles of control items in hoshin kanri. *Standardization and QC* 39 (no. 6) : 7-11 (in Japanese).

Mura, S., ed. 1985. *QC term dictionary.* Tokyo: Japan Standards Association (in Japanese).

Nakamura, Motoichi, and Ishiguro Shigemitsu. 1982. *Ikita senryaku keikaku no tsukuri kata* (Ways to make practical strategic plans). Tokyo: Daiamondo-sha.

Naruge, Shuichi. 1970. *Ningensei shiko* (Toward humanness). Tokyo: Daimondo-sha.

Nayatani, Y. 1978. Use of QC method for hoshin kanri *Quality* 8 (no. 4): 25-31 (in Japanese).

Noda, Y. 1986. Hoshin kanri at Kobayashi-Kosei. *Standardization and QC* 39 (no. 12) : 46-52 (in Japanese).

Nomi, Tokisuke. 1966. Deming plan at Bridgestone Tire Company. *QC* 16 (special fall supplement):173-75 (in Japanese).

_____. 1982. History of Japanese-style quality control. *Hinshitsu gekkan:* 137.

_____. 1982. Special edition: QC diagnosis by top management. *Hinshitsu kanri* (QC) 33 (no. 11-12): 6-48.

_____. 1984. Progress of hoshin kanri: QC problem solving and overall control. *Standardization and QC* 37 (no. 6): 23-40.

_____. 1986. Cautions for hoshin kanri implementation. *Standardization and QC* 39 (no. 12): 4-11 (in Japanese).

Nomi, Tokisuke, et al. 1976. Special edition: How to formulate quality control policies. *Hinshitsu kanri* 27 (no. 1).

_____. 1986. Special edition: Hoshin kanri. *Hyojunka to hinshitsu kanri* 39 (no. 18).

Noya, Y. 1982. *Hoshin kanri for TQC promotion.* Tokyo: Nikka Giren, JUSE (in Japanese).

Ohka, T., S. Nagae, and K. Matsumoto. 1976. Basic concept of production process defects reduction and its company-wide promotion: Target deployment by operation Zercoba. *QC* 27 (November): 95-98 (in Japanese).

Organizing Committee of QC Symposium. 1987. Special features of Japan's companywide QC system: A summary of the 44th QC symposium. *Hinshitsu kanri* 38 (no. 9).

QC Circle Center, ed. 1970. *QC circle principles.* Tokyo: Nikka Giren (in Japanese).

Sagimoto, T., ed. 1986. *QC of clerical, sales, service work.* Tokyo: Japan Standards Association (in Japanese).

Sato, T. 1964. List of control items. *QC* 15 (no. 4): 4-9 (in Japanese).

Schleh, E. C. 1961. *Management by results.* New York: McGraw-Hill. Translated from English by Ueno Ichiro. 1963. *Kekka ni yoru waritsuke keiei.* Tokyo: Ikeda Shoten.

Shimoyamada, Kaoru. 1979. Hoshin kanri at Komatsu *QC* 30 (no. 12): 8-12 (in Japanese).

_____. 1987. A rapporteur's summary of the 44th QC symposium on special features and problems of Japan's QC (part 2). *QC* 38 (no. 7): 60-66 (in Japanese).

Sorokin, P. 1968. Toynbee's historical philosophy: Toynbee study. In *Toynbee's work series*: 41-73. Tokyo: Shakai-Shiso-Sha.

Takamiya, Susumu, ed. 1970. *Shinpan: taikei keieigaku jiten* (Systematic management science dictionary). Tokyo: Daimondo-sha.

Takasu, H., K. Hisazumi, and S. Ito. 1980. Use of control items at this company. *QC* 31 (November, special supplement): 28-32 (in Japanese).

Tamura, Teruichi. 1987. *Ohanashi hoshin kanri* (Discussion of hoshin kanri). Tokyo: Nippon Kikaku Kyokai.

Tokiwa, S. 1979. Hoshin kanri at Ricoh. *QC* 30 (no. 12): 24-28 (in Japanese).

Toynbee, A. J. 1934-39. *A study of history*. Vol. 4. London: Oxford University Press, 120 (in Japanese).

Ueno, Ichiro. 1965. *Mokuhyo ni yoru kanri* (Management by objectives). Tokyo: Ikeda Shoten.

Urabe, Toshimi. 1980. *Keieigaku jiten* (Dictionary of management sciences). Tokyo: Chuo Keizai-sha.

Yamada, Noboru, Tatsuo Sugimoto, and Tokisuke Nomi. 1981. System of total management and hoshin kanri under TQC. Chapter 10 in *Kigyo keiei* (Business management). Keiei Kogaku Series 1. Tokyo: Nippon Kikaku Kyokai.

Yamaguchi, J., T. Sugimoto, and T. Nomi. 1981. *Company management engineering series*. No. 1. Tokyo: Japan Standards Association (in Japanese).

Yoshinobu, J. 1982. *Hoshin kanri to promote TQC*. Tokyo: Nikka Giren (in Japanese).

Yoshinobu, J., et al. 1981. Proceedings of the eighth symposium on hoshin kanri under TQC. Pt. 1. Nippon Hinshitsu Gakkai (in Japanese).

_____. 1982. Proceedings of the tenth symposium on hoshin kanri under TQC. Pt. 2. Nippon Hinshitsu Gakkai (in Japanese).

About the Author/Editor-in-Chief

Born in Japan in 1928, Yoji Akao graduated in 1940 and received his Ph.D. in 1964 from the Tokyo Institute of Technology's Department of Ceramics. He is currently chairman and professor at Tamagawa University's Department of Industrial Engineering. His fields of study include quality control and statistical engineering.

He serves as vice president of the Japanese Society for Quality Control, a member of the Deming Prize Committee (1964-), vice director of the JUSE editorial committee for the *Journal of Statistical Quality Control*, and vice councillor in the head office of QC Circles (1973-).

Dr. Akao's outstanding achievements in his chosen field have been recognized many times, including the Deming Prize in 1978 and the Quality Control Literature Prizes in 1960 for his work in testing defectives and in 1978 for quality function deployment.

Index

Printed in the United States
138701LV00001B/4/P

9 781563 273117